the bathroom
design planner

the **bathroom**
design planner

Vinny Lee & Maggie Stevenson

RYLAND
PETERS
& SMALL

LONDON NEW YORK

Designer Luana Gobbo
Senior Editor Henrietta Heald
Editor Sharon Ashman
Picture Research Claire Hector
Production Tamsin Curwood
Art Director Gabriella Le Grazie
Publishing Director Alison Starling

Illustrations Shonagh Rae

First published in the USA in 2003 by
Ryland Peters & Small, Inc.
519 Broadway
5th Floor
New York, NY 10012

Text pages 6–72, 130–135 and captions throughout by Maggie Stevenson; pages 76–126 and 136–142 by Vinny Lee.

Some of the text in this book appears in *Bathrooms* by Vinny Lee, also published by Ryland Peters & Small.

The authors' moral rights have been asserted.

Printed in China

contents

Library of Congress Cataloging-in-Publication Data

Lee, Vinny.
  The bathroom design planner / Vinny Lee & Maggie Stevenson.
    p. cm.
Includes index.
  ISBN 1-84172-394-0
  1. Bathrooms. 2. Interior decoration. I. Stevenson, Maggie. II.
Title.
  NK2117.B33 L43 2003
  747.7'8--dc21

                    2002014930

introduction

When it comes to bathroom style, anything is possible. But whether your taste is for traditional or modern, the design of this hardworking room must combine comfort, practicality, and good looks in equal measure.

RIGHT **This sleek stone and glass bathroom proves that contemporary style and luxury can fit together perfectly. The room is designed as a wet room— a huge open shower area with an overhead spray. A wide oval bath provides relaxed bathing, while dimmer-controlled lights and built-in speakers create an intimate mood.**

BELOW **In modern bathroom design, nothing is off limits. Ideas and materials once thought suitable only for industrial or commercial settings are now found in home installations. Stainless steel, for example, once used exclusively in the washrooms of hospitals, factories, and prisons, is now an equally strong option for the home.**

Standing under a refreshing shower at the start of the day or slipping into a warm, scented bath at the end of one are so natural to us that it is hard to believe that, until not so long ago, bathing was a weekly chore that was more a necessity than a pleasure. Passionate about invention, engineering, and industry, the British Victorians created the first purpose-made, plumbed-in bathrooms, complete with showers, bidets, and concealed toilet tanks. However, for many decades, these ostentatious fixtures were the exclusive luxury of the very well-off. It was not until the mid-twentieth century that bathrooms became virtually universal, but even then they were chilly places where condensation and cracked linoleum were familiar features.

Now we have learned to love bathing. Vacations in hotels where every room has its own bathroom, visits to health spas where luxury and pampering are guaranteed, and even trips to the gym where powerful showers invigorate tired limbs, have opened our eyes to the possibilities of modern plumbing and raised our ideas of what constitutes the ideal bathroom.

Modern technology and imaginative use of materials have brought about the most radical changes in recent bathroom design. Faucets are more efficient and are available in a wide variety of styles. Showers have powerful pumps and efficient controls to fine-tune the temperature. The conventional three-piece "set" is no longer the only format for bathroom fixtures, nor are ceramic and cast iron the only materials. Walls and floors can be fully waterproofed to create a wet room, or decorated with wallpaper that can now survive in a mechanically ventilated room. Stone or tiled floors can be heated from below and carpets woven from water-resistant synthetic yarns.

These advances may be the product of modern technology, but they expand the design possibilities of contemporary and traditional bathrooms alike, and the real benefits will be found in those areas of bathroom planning that are not defined by style, namely comfort and efficiency.

draw the shape of your bathroom space, adding exact measurements

bathroom
styles

contemporary streamlined,
traditional elegance, country

Once a purely functional room for the weekly chore of bathing, the bathroom is now regarded as a sanctuary—a place in which you can wash away the stresses of the day and luxuriate. The décor reflects the personal tastes of the owners, with the room fitting in with the design of the rest of the home.

BELOW A shower cubicle made from glass bricks combines substance with translucency. Although the bricks allow light through, the glass is obscure enough to provide privacy.

contemporary streamlined

The bathroom is the natural environment for pared-down modern style. Smooth surfaces, technologically advanced fixtures, and a clutter-free space mean that the room looks sophisticated and functions perfectly.

Far from being a chilly, spartan room designed purely for efficiency, a modern streamlined bathroom is more often a soothing space in which to start and end the day. The essence of the look is simplicity, which promotes a sense of calm. Surfaces should be clear, colors quiet, and shapes uncomplicated. Since there are few accessories or decorative details to distract the eye, attention is focused on structural elements. Every imperfection will be visible, so fixtures, materials, and finish must be of the highest quality.

The materials used to create a contemporary streamlined bathroom may be man-made or natural—some of the most successful plans combine the two.

ABOVE Minimalist design relies on the inherent qualities of materials to provide interest. Here, glass and natural stone contrast in exquisitely subtle ways. The sealed plaster wall and limestone tiles are related in color, but one is uniform and the other dappled, while the basin, cabinets, and shower are all made of glass but in different forms.

The list of options includes traditional bathroom materials such as porcelain, enameled cast iron, ceramic, and marble, and migrants from the industrial and commercial world such as stainless steel and glass. Natural substances frequently used in other areas of the home or garden—slate, limestone, and dark oiled wood, for example—have a place in modern bathrooms, as do high quality synthetics such as Corian ® and Lucite ®.

What distinguishes a contemporary streamlined bathroom from any other style is its layout. Ideally, the space will be regular in shape—a simple, seamless shell with nothing to distract the eye from the fixtures, which serve as the dominant features of the room. Spaces that don't conform to this ideal layout can be altered in the most practical way, by converting alcoves and recesses into shower areas, or cupboards with flush doors, which should be decorated to match the walls so they become an extension of them. Uniformity has a way of smoothing out inconsistencies, which is essential for creating the ultimate streamlined look.

ABOVE A rectangular basin on a wide wooden surface or, as here, on a custommade brushed stainless-steel cabinet looks sleek and uncluttered, but a rounded interior allows easy cleaning.

ABOVE LEFT A more open and streamlined look is achieved by choosing fixtures that barely make an impact on the space. Wall-mounted basins and toilets leave the floor area free, while a shallow, purpose-made tiled bathtub, with a glass side panel, has less bulk than a normal one.

The walls and floor are the backdrop against which the bathroom will be arranged, and in addition to setting the style for the room, they must be appropriate to its purpose. All bathroom surfaces should be water tolerant, but the degree to which they need to be depends on how the room is used. The requirements for a family bathroom used by small children, for example, are quite different from those for their parents' connecting room. Similarly, surfaces should be selected according to the amount of exposure to water they must withstand. Hence, the areas around the bathtub and shower need greater water resistance than elsewhere in the room.

Ceramic tiles and mosaics always perform well in wet areas of the home and look good in contemporary bathrooms, as do continuous surfaces such as glass and synthetic stone. Care should be taken with materials like natural stone and wood because, despite their tough, elemental appearance, most wood, some porous stones, and even concrete must be sealed to protect them from water. Generally, wood and water are not a good mix, and laminated wood floors will warp and stain if moisture penetrates their protective surface. However, properly maintained, oily hardwoods such as teak and cedar will shrug off water and can be used for all bathroom surfaces, with the exception of the shower enclosure.

ABOVE **Wood paneling is a traditional wall treatment, but it takes on a modern look when the boards are cut wide and set horizontally. Wood is not generally well suited to the steamy, moist environment of a bathroom but certain hardwoods, such as teak and cedar, have an innate resistance to water. Provided they are anointed periodically with oil, they will maintain their rich natural color for years.**

RIGHT **Stone, wood, and glass share a long history as interior surfaces, and their compatibility remains undimmed. In the bathroom of this country house, wooden furniture and stone walls and floors exist as a tamed reflection of their natural counterparts outdoors, while glass panels allow the sun to slant through the space, enhancing the color and texture of the materials.**

The color scheme for a contemporary bathroom may well be determined by the surface materials used. Wood paneling in suitable wood is inclined to be rich brown, while stone comes in a range of natural tones from off-white to brown and gray. Darker colors look chic and modern teamed with white, while pale neutral tones can create elegant monochromatic schemes.

Light, single-tone schemes are particularly successful in small bathrooms when the continuity of color gives an impression of increased space. They can work equally well—though for different reasons—in larger areas, where a retiring neutral background allows more extrovert designer fixtures to steal the limelight. Positive color also has a place in a contemporary bathroom, creating a lively atmosphere, but the most effective schemes confine themselves to two or three shades. Water-friendly materials that can be used to add color to a bright modern bathroom include ceramic tiles, mosaic, vinyl or rubber flooring, and swimming pool paint.

ABOVE Texture adds interest to neutral schemes with more subtlety than pattern, and the creviced limestone wall in this elegant bathroom contrasts with the smooth shiny surfaces of the ceramic basin on its glossy black bench. Although the stone has been cut, polished, and installed with precision, the random swirl of its grain could not be mistaken for any man-made material.

ABOVE LEFT Stone and wood make a successful marriage in this bathroom, but there has been a reversal of roles. Instead of smooth stone and grainy wood, the wood is smooth to the touch and the travertine deeply fissured. Squared edges give these materials a modern look, and cutting handgrips into the drawer and door fronts leaves the flat surfaces uninterrupted by knobs and handles.

LEFT Darker than most of the stones chosen for interior surfaces, this highly figured brown "mussel" limestone is in danger of appearing dull when used in quantity, but the plain white laminate cabinets and brilliant white paintwork give it a stylish contemporary edge.

BELOW LEFT Parallel lines are a familiar theme in contemporary interiors. In this bathroom they can be seen everywhere—from the countertop and the shelf beneath it to the joints in the mirrored cabinets, the towel radiator, and the grooves incised into the walls and sides of the tub.

BELOW RIGHT The regular vertical grooves cut into the limestone are left rough in contrast to the polished horizontal surface, giving the effect of shadowy light and dark stripes and thus banishing uniformity.

Light is another essential ingredient of the contemporary bathroom. Where possible, the room should be flooded with natural light by day and illuminated with imaginative and functional electric lighting after dark. Bathrooms that lack natural light can be made brighter by installing roof lights, if there is a flat roof above; by replacing part—or all—of a solid wall with a glass partition; or by putting in an obscured glass door in place of a solid wooden one. Inside the room, light can be maximized by employing translucent panels and partitions rather than solid ones and incorporating reflective materials such as mirror and metal in the design. At night, downlighters recessed into the

THIS PAGE **This chunky basin surround is not made of marble, as you might expect, but concrete. Refined, cast, and polished, it proves that industrial materials have a place in modern homes.**

ceiling will light the room dramatically, but task lighting is equally important to create the desired level of illumination needed for detailed activities such as applying makeup or shaving. Enclosed spaces such as shower areas, storage alcoves, and other shady corners need separate lighting.

The choice of sanitary fixtures available for a contemporary bathroom continues to increase, with beautiful sculptural pieces designed by renowned architects and designers like Philippe Starck, Dieter Sieger, and Claudio Silvestrin at the upper end of the price range and simple, stylish shapes from leading chains at more modest prices. The modern bathroom differs from the conventional three- or four-piece set in that, instead of matching components, the layout is likely to focus on one dominant piece—usually the basin or bathtub—with the other items playing a less important role. Often, the basin, toilet, and bidet—if there is one—are wall-mounted to leave the floor clear and conceal the plumbing. This not only gives an impression of space, but it helps to make the room easier to clean.

ABOVE **Mixed and tinted to special recipes, concrete convincingly mimics the texture and color of natural stone. This surround has the satin smoothness of marble, but the soap dish, made to a different formula, possesses the coarse, open grain of pumice.**

Clear, shiny materials are perfect bathroom surfaces. Resisting water but sharing its clarity and reflective quality, they allow light to flood through.

Basins in modern bathrooms are commonly made from white ceramic or glass and sometimes stainless steel. These materials are necessarily rigid and are suitable for round and rectangular shapes, but more unusual materials such as plywood and flexible, translucent PVC lend themselves to more abstract curving shapes. The current trend is for basins to stand on a wide shelf or tabletop, but wall-mounted and under-mounted bowls can look just as sleek.

Although reminiscent of traditional rolltop bathtubs, freestanding tubs are also appropriate for contemporary bathrooms. Instead of ball and

ABOVE LEFT **Large shiny areas of glass, mirror, and glossy surfaces can be disorientating, but the long wooden cabinet provides a visual anchor without dominating the space.**

LEFT AND ABOVE RIGHT **This cylinder of translucent glass is one of a pair of "pods" within an open-plan living area—one is a powder room, the other a shower. The frosted glass makes much less impact than would solid walls, but in order to avoid creating dark shadows the fixtures must be freestanding and plumbed into the floor.**

claw feet, they are more likely to stand on plainly carved wood or stone supports or—in the case of bateau tubs where the exterior sides continue down to the ground—they are placed directly on the floor. Most of these modern freestanding bathtubs are made from acrylic resin and are covered on the outside with the same material or, more exotically, with stainless steel, leather, or even translucent colored plastic, which can be lit from behind. Bathtubs may also be built from natural materials and large, freestanding tubs, custom-made from stone or wood, can form a striking feature in a modern natural bathroom.

A shower is essential in a contemporary bathroom and, where possible, should be separate from the bathtub. If a tub's size and bulk are at odds with the quest for space, it may be dispensed with altogether in favor of a shower. Purpose-made shower enclosures come in a choice of

ABOVE Obscured glass is available in a variety of plain or patterned effects with flat or shiny finishes. Here, the panel screening the basin area presents a polished face and acts as a textural counterpoint to the adjacent concrete wall.

BELOW Glass partitions have the ability to divide space without fragmenting it. Here, frameless curved glass screens enclose and separate the oval tub and shower area, while preserving the view from the wide bow window.

In a contemporary bathroom, fittings like faucets, towel rods, and door handles are selected for their form as well as function.

shapes and sizes, and for a streamlined look, a frameless glass construction is hard to beat. An increasingly popular option is to have a designated shower alcove with waterproofed walls and floor, wall- or ceiling-mounted shower sprays, and a central floor drain. The alcove may be screened with a door or partition wall or, where a sense of total openness is the aim, it can be left exposed to the rest of the room and the surrounding surfaces tanked to render them waterproof, forming a wet room.

The choice of faucets and shower fixtures are important to the style of any bathroom and for contemporary washrooms modern, architect-designed models—and their less expensive copies—abound. Opt for chrome in bright or flat finishes to match the sleek, streamlined look, and choose accessories—such as wall-mounted towel rods, toilet-paper holders, and robe hooks—in similar neat, minimal styles to give a cohesive look.

TOP **A rolltop tub is more at home in a contemporary bathroom when it rests in a stone or wooden cradle.**

ABOVE **Designer faucets have an enduring appeal.**

to achieve the
contemporary look

- **layout**—choose a simple, open-plan design with nothing to distract the eye from the dominant structural elements.

- **surfaces**—go for sleek, smooth materials such as glass, stainless steel, limestone, and man-made options such as Corian.

THIS PAGE **If towels are to dry quickly, adequate rods must be provided so they can be hung individually. By putting a rod along the full length of the countertop where the basins are housed, towels will always be at hand. The steel towel rod echoes the simplicity of the D-line handles on the cupboards below.**

• **fixtures**—select wall-mounted basins, toilets, and bidets to leave the floor clear and conceal the plumbing.

• **accessories**—keep them to a minimum for a totally uncluttered, streamlined space.

• **color schemes**—confine the color to a maximum of two or three shades. Elegant, pale neutral tones and single-tone schemes work well.

• **one dominant fixture**—usually a modern bathtub or basin—serves as the focal point of the room.

traditional elegance

Inspired by the bathrooms of affluent Victorian and Edwardian homes, today's traditional bathrooms are furnished with graceful period fixtures but enjoy the modern luxuries of central heating and hot water on tap.

A traditional urban bathroom exudes luxury and comfort, promising sanctuary and inviting self-indulgence. The style is arguably a high-maintenance one—with surfaces that are not necessarily water resistant and require special care—but it is an easy effect to achieve as both reproduction bathroom fixtures and period items are widely available. The aim is not to recreate a museum piece, authentic in every detail, but to borrow the best from the past and combine it with the comfort and convenience of the present.

Comfort must be the first consideration in a bathroom designed for self-indulgence, and warmth is essential. Heated towel rods, which also warm the room, come in traditional styles with gold or chrome finishes. Old-fashioned cast-iron column radiators are another period option. If inappropriate modern radiators are already installed, they can be concealed inside cabinets. For the ultimate in discreet warmth, consider underfloor heating, which can be installed beneath stone, tile, and in some cases wood flooring, with the only clue to its presence being the luxurious sensation of stepping out of the bathtub onto a warm surface.

Although any bathroom can be designed with a traditional look, the style probably works most successfully in a larger room where there is enough space for a freestanding bathtub to take pride of place. A rolltop tub standing on claw feet is the most popular style of period bath, which can be made even more imposing by decorating the exterior with a faux-marble paint finish or stenciling it—with a laurel garland and monogram, for example.

OPPOSITE An exquisite mosaic floor and elegant architecture set the tone for this luxurious bathroom. High-quality materials such as the deep red marble surround, gold faucets, and mirror-paneled cabinetry complete the scene. An illuminated translucent panel behind the bathtub fills the alcove with a flattering, diffuse light.

BELOW LEFT A complex arrangement of arches and alcoves endows this room with lots of character, but precludes a conventional bathroom layout. Unusual rounded fixtures—some freestanding—have been chosen to harmonize with the architecture without obscuring it.

BELOW RIGHT Even traditional bathrooms can sometimes seem a little clinical, but with the addition of painted walls, soft flooring, and beautiful furniture, the room acquires a warmer and more luxurious atmosphere.

A grand, freestanding bathtub—with claw feet or placed flat on the floor—makes an appropriate centerpiece for a traditional bathroom.

The Empire, or bateau, bathtub is a French alternative to the rolltop. Instead of feet, the Empire tub sits flat on its base, its sides sloping smoothly down from rim to floor, with the upper edge curved so the head and foot are taller than the sides. This style of tub is usually made from enameled cast iron, but antique or reproduction copper versions—polished, lacquered, and adapted for modern plumbing—make a spectacular feature.

In a smaller bathroom, a slipper tub that curves up at one end to facilitate bathing in a semi-sitting position has an authentic period shape but takes up less room than a rolltop or Empire version. At the other extreme, a Victorian canopy bathtub with integral shower surround, complete with overhead rose and body sprays, adds a stately touch to a large bathroom.

To accompany a grand, freestanding bathtub, choose an equally important basin. A porcelain console basin mounted on the wall and supported by two shapely legs at the front is the ideal companion for an Empire bathtub, while a plain white china basin set under the marble top of a converted washstand, sideboard, or chiffonier will make an impressive vanity unit for a Victorian- or Edwardian-style bathroom.

ABOVE LEFT A fine antique bateau bathtub makes a fitting centerpiece for this classical-style bathroom. Raised on a marble plinth and flanked by curved alcoves with trompe l'oeil murals, it is filled by suitably ornate, swan-necked faucets. The modern chairs, with their metal pedestals and transparent seats, provide a striking contrast of style.

ABOVE RIGHT When first made, this copper tub was not intended as a permanent fixture. Originally, it would have been brought out when needed and filled with hot water from the kitchen. Now it occupies the elevated bathing area of a country bedroom and is plumbed with hot and cold water.

The way fixtures are arranged within the bathroom will contribute to the style of the room, and the existing architectural features often suggest a layout. A freestanding bathtub, for example, could be framed in an archway, set in a recess, or placed in front of a fireplace. Alcoves could be used to house a pair of basins or made deeper to accommodate a shower.

If a room has few notable features, it can be made more interesting by raising the tub on a plinth or platform, or creating an alcove for it by positioning it centrally against a wall and building floor-to-ceiling cupboards at each end. A low partition wall could be built to screen the toilet from the bathing area or a full-height one constructed to partially divide the space into separate bathing and dressing areas. Smaller details—such as wood paneling, base boards, picture rails, plaster moldings, and corbels—are relatively easy to install and will add architectural interest and boost the room's period character.

Given that a traditional urban bathroom is likely to be used mainly by adults, it can be decorated with materials like polished wood, marble, and mirror that

BELOW A telephone-style bath/shower mixer is a popular faucet for a traditional bathroom. This one fits on the inside wall of the bathtub, but similar models that fit on the rim of the tub or the wall are also available.

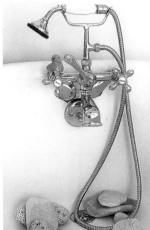

THIS PAGE The exterior of this cast iron tub has been stripped of old paintwork and burnished to give it a bright silvery finish that is slightly uneven as befits its age. The tub is raised on blocks to give it a more dominating presence in this glamorous bathroom.

will remain gleaming and sleek in a comparatively dry and fingermark-free environment. Luxurious floor coverings that might be too slippery, hard, or vulnerable to water for a family bathroom may be perfect for an elegant adult room, and include white marble tiles with black corner pieces, mosaic, parquet, or comfortable—if currently less fashionable—carpet. Walls can be painted or papered, and the wallpaper need not be restricted to the water-resistant but rather utilitarian vinyl kind. As long as there is adequate ventilation to prevent the room from becoming too steamy, ordinary wallpaper will be perfectly serviceable. If the walls are likely to be lightly splashed with water, a coat or two of transparent acrylic glaze will protect the paper, but in areas that need greater water resistance—immediately around the bathtub or behind the basin—shield it with a panel of glass-clear acrylic sheet screwed to the wall.

ABOVE **These built-in cabinets, made from dark polished wood, would fit just as well in a study or living room, but in a classic bathroom they lend a sense of permanence appropriate to the style. The combination of cupboards and drawers offers varied storage for bathroom requisites and conceals the basin plumbing.**

LEFT **A bathtub installed in a bedroom can turn bathing into a congenial affair, and provides a precious opportunity for uninterrupted conversation in a family home. The tub is more easily integrated into the room if it has a stylistic link with the rest of the furniture in it, and the immediate surroundings should be both steam- and splash-resistant.**

Designed to combine the best from the past with modern comforts, today's traditional bathrooms are chic and luxurious.

Shelves and surfaces around the basin are among the most hardworking and must be resistant to impact as well as water, cosmetics, and other preparations used in the bathroom. Glass or ceramic tiles are probably the most practical surfaces and marble the most glamorous—but remember that although it looks tough, polished marble can be etched by spilt perfume, and nail polish may penetrate its porous surface.

Fabrics are rarely used in any quantity in bathrooms because exposure to steam can make them limp and water will mark them, but used judiciously, fabric window treatments make a positive contribution to the room's traditional look. As a rule of thumb, the quantity of fabric may be increased in direct proportion to the size of the room; so in a large airy bathroom, the windows can be dressed with full-length curtains, and in a more compact one, a lambrequin or tailored valance will make a more decorative feature of a window covered by a shade. Between these two extremes, fabric shades—plain or pleated—or windowsill-length curtains are both pretty and practical window treatments.

ABOVE LEFT **One of the best ways to create an authentic-looking period bathroom is to install reclaimed fixtures sourced by a specialist in bathroom antiques. It is rare to find a complete original set, but the juxtaposition of fixtures —mismatched but clearly of the same vintage—adds a quirky and personal twist to the scheme.**

ABOVE RIGHT **Materials, rather than fixtures, are often what gives a room style. This dark paneling creates a masculine, almost cedar-scented air that the modern basin, faucet, and mirror cannot dispel. In a damp room, oiled or sealed hardwoods retain their rich colors.**

In a traditional bathroom, finishing touches like soft, fluffy towels and bowls of dried lavender are a treat for the senses, making the experience of bathing more luxurious.

ABOVE **Original architectural features and structural elements add to the character of a room. Here, an old fireplace has been made into an alcove to hide the plumbing for a bathtub.**

RIGHT **In old houses, an indoor bathroom was often converted from a former bedroom. Here, the fixtures are installed as if they are pieces of furniture.**

An exception to the rule of moderate use of fabric is the shower curtain. One of the most opulent treatments for a rolltop bathtub with an overhead shower is to drape the tub in curtains hung from a ceiling- or wall-mounted rod. The rod can be circular or oval, and the curtains hung from it made from upholstery fabric with a loose, waterproof lining. In use, the fabric curtains will be drawn around the outside of the tub and the waterproof lining hung inside to contain the water.

Aside from the fixtures, the main characteristic of a traditional bathroom is that it is furnished like any other room in the house. A piece of antique furniture transplanted from the bedroom or living room can provide instant period style. A comfortable chair is invaluable for relaxing or dressing, and a gilt-framed mirror and pretty wall lamps will complete the scene.

to achieve the
traditional look

- **materials** throughout the room are of high quality and include marble, polished wood, and mirror.

- **heating** is essential to make the room comfortable—options include heated towel rods, radiators, and underfloor heating.

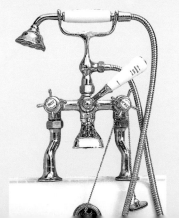

• **fixtures** are of an authentic period style. Use reclaimed or original items if possible, but reproductions are widely available.

• **architectural features** are exploited to work with and help display the fixtures.

• **antique furniture** imported from other rooms in the house, such as dressing tables and cabinets, add to the period style of the bathroom.

• **flooring** is luxurious; consider white marble tiles with black corner pieces, mosaic, parquet, or carpet.

country

Sunlight, fresh air, and the scent of eau de cologne pervade the traditional country bathroom making it the perfect retreat. The fixtures are simple, the design functional, and the atmosphere comfortable.

There are as many styles of country bathroom as there are country homes, but they all have one thing in common—they are modest, simple, and relaxing. At their most successful, they strike a perfect balance between comfort and practicality, but if that balance were to be tipped, it would be toward the functional. Functional in this context should be taken to mean practical rather than austere—the room will be warm in winter, airy in summer, and if it is not overlooked, there will be clear glass in the window with a view that can be admired from the bathtub. The style will be well integrated with the rest of the house, so in a rustic barn remodel, the bathroom will be similarly unrefined while lacking none of the essential facilities; if it is in a large country house, the décor will be quietly elegant; and if it is in a cottage, the scene will be simple with little more than a pile of freshly laundered, fluffy towels and a pot of sweet-smelling flowers to satisfy the senses.

BELOW Exposed structural beams, and wooden window frames and doors inspired the simple style of this country bathroom. The stripped and bleached wood floor and painted tongue-and-groove wainscoting give a plain but warm backdrop for the antique fixtures. The creamy color scheme and a lack of extraneous furniture and accessories could have created a feeling of austerity, but tiny personal details, like the postcard propped on top of the paneling and the perfume bottles, create a relaxed, intimate atmosphere.

LEFT The charm of this bathroom is in the detail. The fixtures are decorative with a distinctively French flavor. Screening the space beneath the basin with a curtain will give an informal, country look to any bathroom.

The bathrooms of many country houses and cottages started out as bedrooms and were converted when the indoor bathroom became an essential part of the home layout. For that reason, they can be spacious and well-proportioned with appealing architectural features, such as an original fireplace or built-in cupboards. The size of the room will have an influence on its style, as spacious rooms can accommodate original turn-of-the-century fixtures that are often larger or more bulky than their modern equivalents.

A rolltop bathtub is a significant feature in any country bathroom, especially if it is placed in the center of the room. Vintage basins tend to be larger and deeper than modern bowls and come

BELOW Paint is the easiest way to refurbish a room while keeping its original features. Here, antique tones of soft white, bone, and ivory have been used.

ABOVE A pastel color scheme creates a relaxed atmosphere. Blue and white are classic bathroom colors, but pink adds a touch of warmth.

LEFT When you're creating a traditional interior, it is always preferable to preserve the original bathroom fixtures than to replace them with reproductions. This built-in double basin is an unusual feature, as is the hinged screen which folds around to give privacy from the glazed door.

BELOW These tiles may have been replaced, but the renovation has been executed with minimal disruption to the existing fixtures. For example, the wooden edging around the shelf has been left intact, and the countertop tiles have been set around the basin without the use of modern plastic sealants.

A country bathroom will be well integrated with the rest of the house, reflecting the style and atmosphere of the other rooms.

in a variety of configurations. In addition to the familiar pedestal and wall-mounted basins, look out for French wrought-iron basin stands, marble-topped washstands that incorporate a basin, double basins, and those designed for special situations like ships' cabins—all of which will add character to a country bathroom. Architectural salvage yards are good hunting grounds for the old and unusual, but the best examples are found only by the most persistent shoppers. Specialized dealers in antique bathrooms charge a little more for their wares but will save you time by offering an edited selection of fixtures and, usually, matching faucets and other brassware.

Not all country bathrooms are large. Some may have been converted from a small storage area while others will have been created in a space partitioned from one of the larger bedrooms.

In such cases, the country look must be tailored to fit. A modern bathtub makes a slimline substitute for an imposing rolltop version and, placed along the wall, will occupy the minimum of floor space. Choose a simple, rectangular shape in white enameled steel or cast iron with few internal contours, and give it country character by boxing it in behind a wood-paneled or tiled surround. To accompany the bathtub, opt for a wall-mounted basin supported on decorative iron brackets or a wooden support. If the space beneath the basin is required for storage, create a vanity unit with wooden paneling to match the bathtub surround, or make a curtain from cotton fabric to fit around the edge of the basin—this will involve building a wooden frame under the basin rim and attaching a curtain track to it.

Good-quality vintage toilets are more difficult to find than other antique bathroom fixtures, but a reproduction version can be integrated into a country bathroom by connecting it to a ceramic high-level tank supported on decorative cast-iron brackets and giving it a dark wood or black Bakelite-style plastic seat and lid.

BELOW LEFT The use of salvaged fixtures is a sure way of introducing traditional country style into a powder room. To exploit the limited space in this compact bathroom, the resourceful owner installed fixtures taken from a yacht. Emphasizing the height of the room helps to detract from the restricted floor area and the tall, narrow mirror over the basin and the high shelf encourage the eye upward.

BELOW RIGHT This blue-veined bowl inspired a blue and white color scheme. Striped towels and a shell-shaped soap dish reinforce the nautical theme.

Architectural salvage yards are good hunting grounds for old and unusual fixtures—French wrought-iron basin stands, double basins, and items designed for special situations—all of which will add character to a country bathroom.

ABOVE In a space where the structure of the building has been left visible, it would be hard to construct a domesticated bathroom. The alternative is to focus on the essentials—a freestanding bathtub and a table to hold bathing items, placed against a backdrop of dramatic color.

RIGHT This Scandinavian-style country bathroom skillfully combines old and new. The table and stool show visible signs of age, but the antique rolltop tub has been fully restored. The tiled floor, paneling, and window treatment are pristine, but their simple design means they fit in with their rustic setting.

FAR RIGHT Found materials create the decoration for this idiosyncratic bathroom. The walls are clad with a light-reflecting mosaic made from fragments of mirror and glass, and a slice of corrugated zinc acts both as a support for a shelf and a rack from which to hang accessories.

Sometimes, the space available for a bathroom is so limited that it is more practical to forego the tub completely and create a shower room instead. Purpose-made shower cubicles are invariably modern or urban in design, so the alternatives open to the country-style shower room designer are to build a tiled shower enclosure with partition walls or to create a wet room. The latter may seem more suited to a modern town house, but fully waterproofed shower rooms with a floor drain to carry away the water are a common feature of country homes throughout southern Europe. The principal difference is in the style. Unlike sleek glass- or stone-lined urban wet rooms, the country version will be fully tiled—with plain white or colored

LEFT It is unusual to find a wet room in a traditional interior, but in this wedge-shaped attic bathroom, with insufficient space for a tub or conventional shower enclosure, it offers a practical solution. The white-tiled room is filled with light from the bare windows, and the period-style basin and shower fixture are a discreet presence barely intruding on the space. The dark tiled floor, by contrast, provides a dramatic anchor.

tiles—and the shower itself a classic overhead rose. The experience of using such a shower will also be different—standing in a generous but gentle downpour of water in contrast to the sharp, invigorating body jets of a contemporary power shower.

Fully tiled walls are rarely seen in a country bathroom except in a shower area, but where they are used to protect surfaces around the bathtub or behind the basin, they are distinctively rustic or nostalgic in style. Hand-made Mediterranean or Mexican tiles have the right degree of informality, and a collection of odd, unmatched Victorian tiles arranged in a random patchwork evokes a sense of the past. An alternative to tiles is tongue-and-groove wainscoting, which can be used to enclose the tub, to build a vanity unit around the basin, and, as a dado, to protect the walls from splashes. Usually, it is painted with eggshell paint to give a semi-matt,

ABOVE Highly glazed tiles with concentric rope twist borders in rich jewel colors define the shape of this shower room. The floor must be fully waterproof, continue up the perimeter walls to form a leak-free seam where the two planes meet, and have a gentle slope to make sure the water flows to the drain.

Sealed with varnish or durable floor paint, original floorboards make a suitably rustic floor covering for a country bathroom.

ABOVE An eclectic assortment of furniture brings comfort to this tiny bathroom. The cabinet, from a 1950s kitchen, focuses storage in a compact space, and the wicker chair folds up and slides neatly into the space at the end of the tub when not in use.

wipeable finish that wears well. Elsewhere, wall surfaces tend to be flat white, tinted pastel, or rich earthy colors. Paint is the obvious medium for this, and special latex paints are now available that can withstand a steamy bathroom.

The floor covering in any bathroom must be water resistant, resilient, and easy to clean. Linoleum fulfills all these criteria, has the right period credentials, and comes in a wide choice of colors. Laminated or veneered wood flooring is best avoided; it can be damaged by moisture, and its immaculate, smooth appearance is out of keeping with the rustic feel of the setting. Original floorboards are a different matter since the narrow gaps between them allow enough air flow for spills and splashes to dry naturally. To make sure they are comfortable and safe to walk on, the boards should have all nails hammered down and be stripped and sealed or painted with durable floor paint.

to achieve the
country look

- **fixtures**—period or salvaged basins and rolltop bathtubs are ideal, but slimline tubs can work well in smaller rooms, boxed in behind a wood-paneled surround.

- **flooring**—linoleum or floorboards set the scene; both are resilient and easy to clean.

THIS PAGE Items from other rooms in the house give this pretty bathroom a lived-in look. The marble-topped table on cast iron legs may once have occupied a conservatory, the wooden framed mirror may have hung in a hall, and the wirework wastepaper basket probably spent its early years in an office.

• **walls**—often painted with white, pastel, or earthy colors; otherwise, tongue-and-groove paneling or rustic-style tiles can be used to cover the walls.

• **storage**—increase the amount you have by screening the space beneath the basin with a pretty curtain, or by constructing a vanity unit using wooden paneling to match the bathtub surround.

• **furniture**—use an eclectic mix of simple, rustic pieces, including treasures from flea markets and other found items.

style notes

bathroom
planning

a guide to perfect planning; case studies
focusing on large, medium-sized, and
the most compact of bathrooms

Today's bathroom is an increasingly important room—and careful planning is essential to creating a design that fulfills all your needs. This chapter looks at six rooms of various shapes and sizes, and highlights the inventive ways in which the different spaces have been used and, in some cases, transformed.

planning and installing

Whether you are installing a brand-new bathroom or remodeling an existing one, careful planning will help you tailor your ideas to suit both your lifestyle and your budget.

Everyone has their own picture of the perfect bathroom, and with enough space and a generous budget anything is possible. But for most of us there are restrictions, and given that this room is one of the most expensive and disruptive to install, a new bathroom must be carefully planned.

One of the best ways to begin the planning process is to identify the role of your new bathroom. Will it be a connecting or a family bathroom? Will it be used by more than one person at a time? Do you like to bathe quickly or in a leisurely way? Will any of those using the bathroom be very young or elderly? Do you want it to double as a dressing room? Do you need storage only for toiletries or for towels and cleaning products as well? Think about style, too. Do you favor a modern or traditional look? Does the design need to integrate into an adjoining room? These questions will help you decide your priorities.

ABOVE LEFT **There's no reason why a family bathroom should not be glamorous, and here a pair of elegant console basins mean that washing and teeth cleaning can be performed communally and in style.**

ABOVE RIGHT **Warmth and intimacy seem to be part and parcel of a traditional bathroom. Perhaps it is the rounded shapes of the tub and column radiator or the relaxed purity of its simple decoration that make this one so inviting.**

LEFT, BELOW, AND BOTTOM
A connecting bathroom
need not be separated by
solid walls. In this
bedroom, a basin and tub
are placed along one wall
and partially screened by
translucent partitions.
These protect furnishings
from water splashes and
are sufficiently obscured to
allow privacy for washing
and showering while also
allowing conversation
when both partners are
using the room at the same
time. The bathtub has been
built into a surround that
gives the enclosure greater
width and provides a shelf.

If you are refurbishing a bathroom, list what you like and dislike about the existing one. You will be able to avoid many of the faults in the old design, but take care not to sacrifice any of its good features, and be prepared to compromise on the things that can't be changed.

Next, decide what fixtures you want. The minimum for a conventional bathroom is a basin, toilet, and tub, but there are many variations. In a household with one bathroom and two or more members of the family who leave home together, twin basins will ease the morning rush. For many, a bath is a necessity, but in a small bathroom the tub could be exchanged for a shower enclosure to save space or, for a real feeling of openness, the room could be designed as a wet room—fully waterproofed and with no partitions around the shower area. If you want both a bath and shower, the choice is

between separate fixtures or an over-tub shower. A separate shower that you can walk in to is easier to use than an over-bath shower, but in a smaller room this convenience may be at the cost of overcrowding and a choice must be made. In some places, every well-appointed bathroom contains a bidet, while in others it is an optional extra. Ultimately, it is a question of personal preference and pressure on space.

The fixtures you choose will depend on the style you want and your budget. Generally, top-quality fixtures with designer labels are expensive but there are plenty of good-looking alternatives in affordable lines. Compare styles and prices by visiting bathroom showrooms and looking through brochures.

Sometimes it is feasible to increase the size of the bathroom by moving an internal wall and stealing space from an adjoining room.

ABOVE A wide basin is useful for activities that require extra space, such as shaving. This one is an unusual wall-mounted model with a high upstand at the back that integrates the faucets.

THIS PICTURE In a small bathroom ducting has been built along one wall to hold the toilet tank and basin. The custom-made trough-shaped double bowl has been mounted under the thick countertop.

The best way to decide whether your chosen fixtures will fit into the available space is to draw a scale floor plan of the room and elevations of each wall on graph paper; then cut out cardboard shapes representing the various fixtures to the same scale. Manufacturers' brochures will give you the exact sizes of their products. On your floor plan and elevations, mark all permanent features such as windows, doorways, and the opening arcs of the doors. Next, place the cutouts of the fixtures on the floor plan, moving them around until you find a feasible layout. Remember to leave enough space around them for comfortable use. Bathtubs need a strip at least 3 feet (90cm) wide alongside to allow bathers to step out and dry themselves, while showers need a space 28in (70cm) wide. Basins require 28in (70cm) in front and 8in (20cm) at each side; the toilet and bidet need 24in (60cm) in front and 8in (20cm) at the sides. If the room will be used by one person at a time, these

ABOVE Daylight is the best light for detailed tasks, and a window at right angles to the mirror gives brightness without glare. Additional lighting is supplied by the illuminated mirror, which has a circle of light to frame the reflection.

ABOVE LEFT Most of the fixtures in this bathroom have been custom-made in stainless steel. This metal can look dull and gray, so the lighting scheme has been designed to reflect on it and highlight its gleaming surface. A skylight over the bathtub illuminates its curved interior; fiber optic lights in the shower head transform the spray into a dazzling light show, and lights hidden behind curved steel baffles shine on the basin and mirror.

When tackling the plumbing and electrical elements, be aware of the pros and cons of different systems and the main safety requirements.

access areas can be overlapped slightly to save space, but conversely family bathrooms used by two or more people simultaneously will need extra space for the users to pass each other. In attic bathrooms, you will need to allow enough headroom where fixtures are situated under sloping ceilings.

As you arrange the fixtures on your graph paper floor plan, refer to the elevations to make sure there is no conflict with doors, windows, or radiators. If necessary, doors can be re-hung or moved, and radiators moved or replaced by underfloor heating to make difficult layouts possible.

Budgeting for a new bathroom is not always a matter of adding up the prices of the fixtures and adding the cost of installation. Some design ideas carry hidden costs that can stall your plans. For example, departing from the original plan of an existing bathroom may require plumbing to be re-routed. An especially large tub, when full of water, will be much heavier than a standard one, and the floor may need to be strengthened to support its weight.

Whatever the estimated cost of your new bathroom, always allow a little extra for unforeseen expenses and for the all-important finishing touches.

ABOVE LEFT **When planning a bathroom layout, leave enough space around the fixtures for them to be used comfortably and to allow easy cleaning. A minimum gap of 8in (20cm) should be left on both sides of the toilet.**

ABOVE RIGHT **Twin basins are intended to be used at the same time and need extra surrounding space to give both people room to move freely. For safety, bathroom radiators can be boxed into specially designed cabinets that allow the heat to circulate but prevent hot bars from touching bare skin.**

budget **checklist**	estimated **cost**
preparatory plumbing and electrical work	
miscellaneous building works: preparing floors and walls	
installation of fixtures and built-in furniture	
flooring	
lighting	
decorating	
ceramic tiles	
built-in units	
freestanding cupboards, cabinets, and shelving	
heated towel rod	
exhaust fan	
fixtures:	
basin	
bathtub	
toilet	
bidet	
shower door/enclosure	
shower tray	
shower fixture	
faucet	
accessories, such as mirror, soap dish, toothbrush holder	
other items	
total	

THIS PAGE **Designed with efficiency, this bathroom is fitted with enough storage to contain clothes as well as bathroom requisites. Light oak walls and cabinets and details like the wood moldings and silver-framed mirror give the room a sleek and sophisticated look. A glass countertop, impervious to water or cosmetics, makes a practical but luxurious surface for the vanity unit.**

large dual-purpose bathroom

A large bathroom that doubles as a dressing room provides a private space in which to prepare for the day or wind down at the end of it.

A dressing room is a luxury few enjoy, but a larger-than-average bathroom can easily be converted for the purpose. To fulfill both activities, the room must incorporate all the usual bathroom fixtures together with a well-lit vanity area and generous amounts of storage for both bathroom needs and clothes. As with any dual-purpose room, it is essential to segregate the things that are best kept separate, such as showering and clothes storage, and to arrange the fixtures in a logical order of use.

This bathroom lends itself to dual-purpose use very well. It has a large window at one end and a second, smaller one in the side wall so, by day, the entire space is filled with natural light. To make it work better as a combined bathroom and dressing

Although the room has been divided into two separate areas, the design succeeds in maintaining a sleek, clean look and uncluttered feel.

room, the space is divided by sliding glass doors that can be drawn aside to give a continuous open space or pulled across to offer some privacy. To define the areas of activity further, there is a change of floor level that allows some of the pipework to be concealed under the raised floor and reduces the height of the bathing area, inducing a sense of intimacy.

The room is divided so the bathroom area is a little smaller than the dressing room. Although it is still a comfortable size, space has been used with economy and the bathtub, toilet, and a built-in bench are the only permanent fixtures. In the interests of retaining an open aspect, an over-tub shower was installed instead of a separate shower enclosure. To emphasize the clean and uncluttered look, the walls, floor, side of the tub, and bench are all covered with limestone, providing a continuous, water-resistant surface that is both practical and elegant.

The other part of the room is devoted to grooming and dressing, with a wide, built-in vanity unit and tall closet filling one side of the room. A thick

RIGHT **Stainless steel is a versatile material. Usually chosen for functional and contemporary interiors, here a polished steel bowl integrates into an eclectic setting that successfully combines a traditional mirror and faucets with a modern glass countertop.**

BELOW **This bathroom-dressing room is large enough to allow separate zones for the different activities. Bathing and showering are confined to the farthest section of the room, with dividing doors and efficient air extraction controlling the level of humidity. The remaining section is planned with ample storage space.**

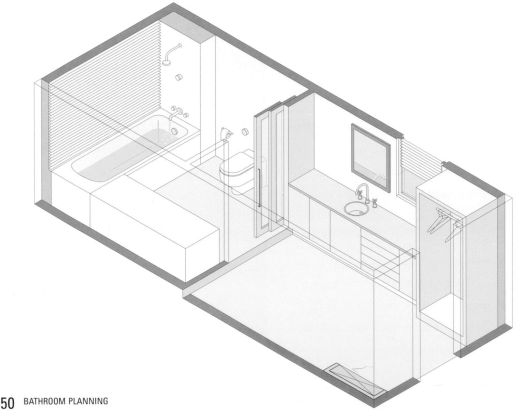

ABOVE **The beauty of custommade cabinets is that they can be fitted with compartments to keep the contents neat—in this case, to divide socks according to color.**

BELOW **A faux ivory-handled razor and shaving brush indicate that the owner of this bathroom inclines more to traditional taste than contemporary.**

glass countertop runs the full length of the vanity unit and is punctuated by a round stainless-steel basin. Below it, light oak cupboards and drawers accommodate clothes, toiletries, and cosmetics. The closet is actually a doorless hanging space with two-tier rails for shirts and trousers. Opposite is a second tall cabinet, this time with shelving to hold perfectly folded towels. The wood-paneled walls in this part of the room contribute to the atmosphere of calm and sophistication, and a sisal rug softens the stone floor adding to the sense of comfort and warmth.

large minimalist bathroom

There are two ways of dealing with a large space—you can fill it or simply appreciate it. The owner of this bathroom has achieved a sense of serenity by choosing minimal fixtures and celebrating the space and light.

THIS PAGE Where better to relax and restore your equilibrium than in a tub of scented water, gazing up through a skylight to a clear blue sky? One of the most seductive qualities of this bathroom is that it is drenched in natural light, which flatters the golden limestone, creating a sense of warmth and wellbeing.

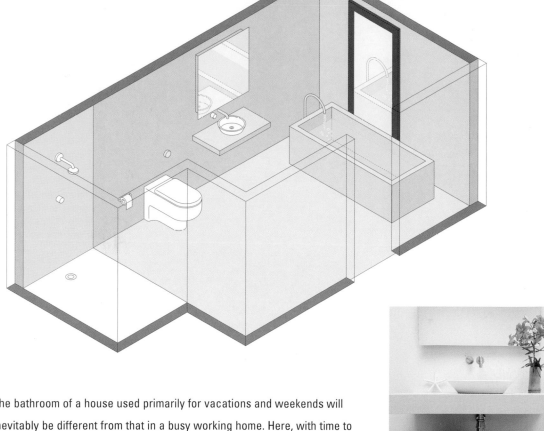

The bathroom of a house used primarily for vacations and weekends will inevitably be different from that in a busy working home. Here, with time to spare and no immediate pressures, bathing can be a relaxing experience to be savored, and for the owner of this bathroom, space was essential to creating a haven of tranquility far removed from the bustle of the city.

The owner retained the footprint of the previous occupants' bathroom but discarded their glamorous style for her own, more restrained taste. Convinced that an uncluttered environment helps to clear the mind, she stripped back the room to the shell and then refitted it with the barest essentials. By employing only the most beautiful materials and carefully chosen fixtures in colors selected from a pale, neutral palette, the result is not cold and unfriendly but serenely minimal.

Stone is the predominant material used in the room, and the particular type of stone—Wisconsin limestone—is similar in appearance to French limestone, with a warm color, faintly veined with gold and touches of gray. The stone covers the floor, lines the shower area, and forms the bathtub and a vanity shelf for the basin. Lit from above by twin skylights, the stone, brightened by the white walls, glows with a soft radiance.

TOP **This bathroom is large by any standards with a main floor area of 20ft x 8ft (6m x 2.5m) and a shower area 4ft x 5ft (1.2m x 1.5m). A small curb that separates the shower from the rest of the room also helps to contain the water.**

ABOVE **No conventional provision has been made for storage, the owner preferring a more flexible alternative of wicker boxes and a large bowl.**

LEFT **Chosen for their pure, sculptural shapes, the basin and toilet show that fixtures from separate lines made by different manufacturers can be combined successfully.**

BELOW AND BOTTOM **There are deliberately few accessories to disturb the pure, minimal style of the room, and those that are displayed—starfish and sponges—have a natural affinity with the pale stone that dominates the room.**

To maintain the simplicity of the room, accessories are strictly limited, as is storage, and there are no extraneous pieces of furniture.

Although the design of the room is resolutely understated, the fixtures are striking in their simplicity. The wall-mounted toilet and the shallow basin—resting on its cantilevered stone shelf—seem to float weightlessly above the floor, while the stone tub appears to have grown out of the ground. The tub was built on site by a swimming-pool maker, skilled in the ways of joining stone with waterproof seams. Such a large object required light and space to balance its bulk. Placed away from the wall and under a skylight, it stands as a sculptural presence.

THIS PAGE This bathroom offers generous facilities for both showering and bathing. The tub was custom-made from the same stone that features elsewhere in the room. Larger and deeper than an ordinary bathtub, it is a straight-sided, rectangular edifice made in proportion to the room and is its most imposing feature. Bathing in it is more like stress therapy than an act of ablution. The tub is filled by a simple spout rising straight from the floor.

THIS PAGE **To aid the passage of light from the window to the far end of the room, the walls and floor have been tiled in off-white, with touches of green to add a note of freshness. The door is paneled with mirror, which helps to maximize light and make the room seem wider.**

elongated elegance

A well-planned layout and some clever design tricks stretch the visual limits of a compact room.

Planning a bathroom is not just a matter of placing all the necessary fixtures like pieces in a jigsaw: there must be enough room for them to be used easily while leaving enough remaining free space to convey a feeling of openness. This extra spaciousness makes the room seem less cluttered and more relaxed but, more practically, also makes it more convenient to use—it allows you to climb out of a bath and towel dry without standing dangerously close to a hot radiator or splashing clean clothes with drops of water.

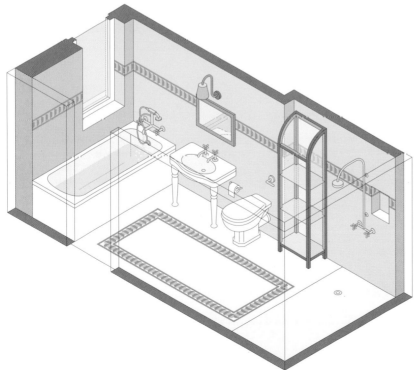

ABOVE **A wide porcelain console basin in the French style helps to fill the central part of the room without crowding it, while the looking glass above it faces the mirror on the door to produce infinitely repeating reflections. The bell-shaped wall lamp provides direct light for the basin.**

LEFT **This bathroom is more than twice as long as it is wide, and a difficult shape to plan. It also suffers from a lack of daylight. By concentrating interest and light in the center, the room seems wider, brighter, and more spacious than it is.**

A pale color scheme enhances the little daylight the room receives.

Some bathrooms may have adequate space, but the arrangement can make planning the room difficult, and this one, in a city apartment building, is a good example—a lofty corridor of a room, lit by a small window at one end. The difficulties of an awkward shape and insufficient daylight have equal impact on the way the room feels, but short of moving walls or enlarging the window, both problems had to be solved by imaginative design and decoration.

To enhance the daylight, a pale scheme was chosen with off-white tiles covering the floor, bath housing, and walls. A tall, narrow space never feels completely comfortable, so to reduce the perceived height of the room, the wall tiles were stopped short of the ceiling, and the effect was consolidated by the addition of a border of green and white tiles that encircles the walls at picture-rail level. Drawing down the eye level this way not only detracts from

ABOVE **A glass cabinet that previously served as a shop display case is now home for a collection of scent bottles and brilliant green glass, chosen to match the border tiles.**

ABOVE LEFT **A tall ceiling can make a bathroom seem austere, but incorporating a patterned border into the tiling at picture rail height helps to lower the sight line, visually reducing the height of the room. The ceiling light has also been lowered to illuminate the lower part of the bathroom.**

Clever use of a colored tile border has the effect of widening the room.

ABOVE **A traditional soap holder hooks over the rim of the bath. The enameled holder is pierced with a stylized petal pattern to allow water to drain away.**

ABOVE LEFT **A simple but efficient shower mixer delivers a deluge of water through a large fixed rose. A storage cubbyhole is recessed into the wall at one side—the tile border dipping in and out of it, uninterrupted in its progress around the room.**

the height of the room, but the emphatic horizontals make it seem wider, too. The same border was used on the floor with an infill of the same design to form a tile "rug," creating a focus at the center of the room.

To reduce the apparent length of the bathroom, the tub was placed across its width at one end, and an open shower area across it at the other. To link the two, the fixtures were ranged along one long wall between them. This also served to give an impression of space at the center of the room, which is accentuated by putting mirrors on opposite sides of the room and rehanging the door to open out. To make the most of the daylight, the window is left uncovered except for a gauze curtain covering the lower sash. A light suspended in the center of the room and a pretty wall lamp over the basin form a pool of light, again drawing attention to the central area of the room.

medium-sized bathroom on a budget

The design of this bathroom was determined more by budget than space.
It contains all the essential fixtures without wasting any room.

Presented with the freedom to decide the size and shape of every room in
the apartment, the owner of this former warehouse space had to prioritize.
Devoting more room to the bathroom would mean depriving the kitchen or
living room of space, but making it too small for comfort or convenience
would be a lasting irritation.

**BELOW LEFT The wall to the
right of the tangerine door
is made from corrugated
plastic, obscure enough
to provide privacy but
sufficiently translucent
to allow daylight to spill
through to the living space.**

In an industrial building, the architecture influences the layout, and the
large volume must be carefully managed if the central area is to receive any
natural light from windows in the exterior walls. Occupying the space in front
of one of these windows, the bathroom had to be designed with this in mind.

Instead of filling this bathroom to capacity, the designer included only the
basic fixtures, leaving enough clear space for drying and dressing. There is no

**ABOVE Available in a
choice of profile widths,
corrugated plastic roofing
sheet makes an innovative
translucent bath panel.**

THIS PAGE **Opening directly onto the living area, the bathroom is an integral part of a universally brilliant color scheme. The flooring continues the blue theme throughout the entire space. By shopping at building supply outlets for good-quality, classic fixtures in standard sizes, and using unconventional materials with flair, the designer has created a stunning bathroom within the very tight budget.**

separate shower enclosure, but a tub with an over-tub spray allows for
soaking and showering in one compact space. A wall-mounted basin leaves
the floor clear, while the toilet has its plumbing hidden within a false wall,
giving the room a streamlined profile. Storage exists in the form of a recess
carved into the false wall with mirrored panels that slide across to conceal it.

ABOVE **Cheap faucets are
a false economy; changing
them later will be both
expensive and disruptive.
Instead, seek high-quality
water fixtures from good
plumbing suppliers.**

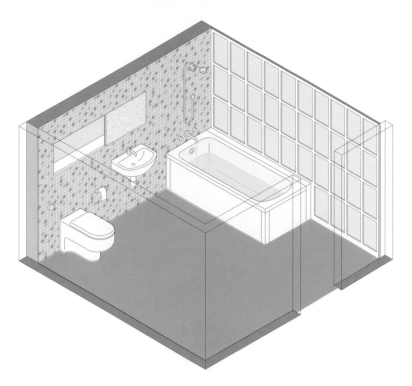

Instead of filling this bathroom to capacity, the designer included only the basic fixtures, leaving enough clear space for drying and dressing.

The arrangement of the fixtures is unconventional. One of the original metal-framed warehouse windows fills the whole of one wall, but instead of leaving the glass uncovered to take advantage of the light, the bathtub has been placed across it. The level of light has not been too much reduced, however, as imaginative use of translucent corrugated plastic in the form of a bath panel allows it to flow under the tub and into the room. The same material has been used to build the partition dividing the bathroom from the living area, so light from the same window filters through the whole space.

FAR LEFT In keeping with larger items in the bathroom, translucent materials have been used for smaller accessories like this laundry hamper. The semitransparent plastic makes the rising level of laundry visible without removing the lid, and the hamper can be easily washed to keep it fresh.

LEFT The storage recess is deep enough to hold spare towels as well as jars and bottles. In contrast to the tiled walls, the interior is painted white to provide a smooth surface that is easy to wipe clean. The narrow rim of the opening forms a neat frame for the mirror when the doors are closed.

clever small bathroom

Lack of space is so common in a bathroom that it barely registers as a design challenge. With careful use of color and a bit of ingenuity, a cramped bathroom can be transformed into an airy space.

The bathroom in a good hotel demonstrates how successful a small bathroom can be. Rarely larger than is absolutely necessary, it contains all the essentials, yet by adopting a streamlined layout and employing only top-quality fixtures and surfaces, it still feels luxurious. The home bathroom differs from this only in its need to include adequate storage.

This tiny bathroom in a small city apartment was redesigned as part of a major refurbishment. The owner wanted to open up and brighten the space, replacing the old furnishings with clean lines and a cool color scheme. The bathroom is sandwiched between the bedroom and living room with doors opening into both rooms. As it had become a convenient through route, it was decided to keep both doors, but this meant retaining the same basic layout.

ABOVE **The two doors in this room reduce the space available for wall-mounted accessories, but by putting towel rods one above the other, the storage potential of this wall is doubled.**

ABOVE LEFT **Situated between the bedroom and living room, the bathroom serves as a short cut between the two. Black granite thresholds separate the pale bathroom floor from the dark polished oak in the other rooms.**

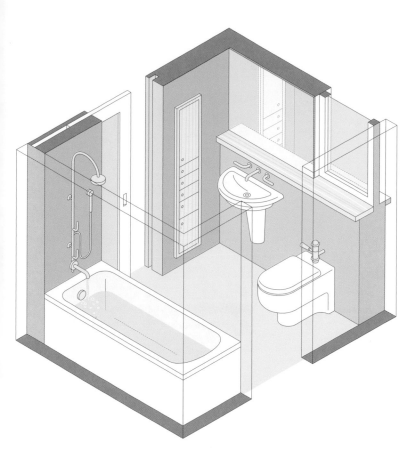

LEFT **Measuring 5ft x 8ft
(1.5m x 2.4m), with doors
in two facing walls, the
bathroom needed careful
planning to make the best
use of the space available.
The thickness of the wall at
the head of the bathtub was
increased considerably to
accommodate the pocket
doors, the built-in storage
cabinet, and the plumbing
for the shower.**

BELOW **Pocket doors
that slide back inside the
adjoining wall replaced
the old hinged doors. Their
panels are mirrored on the
bathroom side to provide a
full-length looking glass.**

To make better use of space and give a more streamlined look both inside and outside the bathroom, the existing hinged doors were replaced with sliding pocket doors. Unlike track-mounted doors, which slide over the wall they open onto, pocket doors are fitted in double-thickness walls and, when open, disappear into the space between the leaves of the wall. To accommodate the doors, the walls on both sides of the bathroom were made thicker and, in order to contain the plumbing to the shower and a built-in storage unit, the wall between the bedroom and bathroom was increased to a thickness of almost 1ft (30cm).

To achieve a clear floor area—and to give a greater feeling of space—it was decided that the fixtures and storage should be wall mounted. The double-thickness walls proved a valuable asset in this respect since a great deal of storage could be recessed into them. To the left of the basin, a purpose-made

THIS PAGE Designed to
give a thorough overhead
drenching as well as more
controlled rinsing, the
shower fixture has a large
fixed rose and a smaller
hand-held spray. By ending
the area of tiling short of
the ceiling and edging it
with a "picture rail" of
square aluminum tube,
the ceiling line is visually
lowered, and the horizontal
stretch of the upper wall
is accentuated, giving the
room an impression of
greater space.

Improved plumbing and specially designed fixtures mean that there is no reason why compactness should preclude efficiency and elegance.

vertical cabinet in bleached ash contains a series of drawers for make-up, a tilting wastebasket, and a compartment with electrical outlets. Open shelves are recessed into the wall at the foot of the tub, and, on the other side of the doorway, surface-mounted rods in two tiers hold the towels.

The basin, a wall-mounted bowl with a ceramic trap cover to conceal the plumbing, has an integral rail below to hold hand towels and a glass shelf above. On the same wall, a medicine cabinet is camouflaged within a longer mirrored panel. Measuring just 28in (70cm) wide, the bathtub is the narrowest available and fits snugly into the alcove at one side of the room.

Light plays an important part in creating an illusion of space, and here a combination of pale colors and mirrored surfaces works the deception.

ABOVE To blend with the overall pale scheme of silvery blue, bleached ash has been used for the storage cabinet. Storage space is supplemented by the mirrored medicine cabinet above the basin.

ABOVE LEFT The built-in cabinet provides a lot of storage in a small space. It contains a series of small cupboards and drawers or pull-out trays that can be removed to give easy access to their contents.

a small bathroom reinvented

Moving interior walls sounds like drastic action, but where the design of a bathroom is limited as much by its shape as its size, reordering the layout of the room is a practical solution.

A shower is a requirement in any contemporary bathroom, but only a minority would choose it in preference to a tub. The ideal is to have both. When this long, narrow bathroom was revamped, a shower was high on the owners' list of priorities, but the shape of the room made it difficult to install a standard-sized enclosure, let alone the very large shower lined with bright, Moroccan-style tiles they hankered after.

Unfazed by the restrictions of the layout of the interior walls, designer Audrey Carden of Carden Cunietti looked outside the bathroom for potential space for annexation and found it in the adjoining dressing room. The planned shower—a large,

ABOVE Built from maple with Shakerlike simplicity, the basin stand is given a plain frieze to conceal the underside of the basin and the plumbing.

RIGHT Lack of space in the original bathroom led to the ingenious idea of hollowing a shower area out of the dressing room next door.

LEFT The shower enclosure is a large curved space, perfect for energetic showering. A section of the wall is built from glass bricks to allow daylight to enter from the dressing room beyond, while spotlights recessed into the ceiling provide additional light in the evening. Raised above the level of the bathroom floor, the base of the shower dips gently at the center to allow water to flow into a floor drain.

horseshoe-shaped area enclosed by full-height walls—was built within the floor plan of the dressing room, and then a doorway was made through the dividing wall to give access from the bathroom. Had it been totally surrounded with solid walls, the new shower area would have needed constant artificial light, but by constructing the curved rear wall of frosted glass bricks, daylight is allowed to pass freely from the dressing room to illuminate the enclosure.

The main part of the bathroom retained its original long, narrow shape, but was visually reproportioned by centering the basin on one short wall and placing the tub along the other. Mounting the tub underneath a broad limestone rim had the effect of widening the bathtub—and therefore

ABOVE Blue and red mosaic tiles, arranged in a zigzag pattern across the floor of the shower area, look like an oriental carpet. The same blue tiles cover the walls, metallic ones dotted among them glinting like fish scales in the light.

LEFT Maple paneling, a tone darker than the limestone floor, extends the area of pale neutral color in the lower part of the room, visually expanding the floor space. A wall-mounted shelf and a broad limestone ledge around the bathtub provide areas for storage and display.

RIGHT The basin is part of a symmetrical arrangement, with a mirror centered above it and matching lamps on the sides.

BELOW Sometimes small details influence the style of a room to a degree that is out of proportion to their size. This Moroccan dish —used as a soap dish— with its vibrant blue color and zigzag pattern, is a microcosm of the shower enclosure design.

Mounting the tub underneath a broad limestone rim had the effect of widening the bathtub.

shortening the room even more—and the wooden paneling put in horizontally exaggerates the width of the room.

Above the maple dado, the walls are painted in striking contrast with an intensely vibrant blue, high-pigment theatrical paint. The color effectively links the brilliantly tiled shower alcove with the rest of the room, invigorating what would otherwise be a pale, neutral scheme and reinforcing the Moroccan theme.

sketch a layout for your bathroom, showing fixtures

surfaces &
lighting

tiled, glass, stone, and wood walls;
cork, rubber, linoleum, vinyl, stone, and
wood flooring; task and ambient lighting

Seamless and streamlined, or colorful and detailed—the surfaces with which you choose to cover your floors, walls, and surrounds will have an enormous impact on the feel of your bathroom. Likewise, lighting has the power to create an atmosphere—whether it is calm and relaxing or purely functional.

walls and surrounds

Glass, stone, wood, and plaster are sought-after materials for walls and surrounds in modern bathroom schemes. These organic surfaces work well both with ordinary white fixtures and with hard steel finishes.

Traditionally, the areas of a bathroom that came into regular contact with water were tiled, and the rest of the room was either painted or hung with vinyl-coated wallpaper. Today's schemes include a much wider variety of surfacing materials, including glass—which appears in all sorts of imaginative guises—and plaster, stone, and wood, whose tactile and earthy finishes soften the sometimes aggressive lines of modern bathroom fixtures.

Glass can be plain or opaque, colored or clear, but it should be used in a bathroom only if it has been laminated or toughened. Lamination involves sandwiching liquid resin between two sheets of glass. If one sheet of the laminated glass breaks, the other remains intact and most of the shattered glass remains attached to the sheet. Toughened glass is heat-treated to make it four times more durable than standard glass. If it breaks, it crumbles into

ABOVE LEFT Ceramic tiles are a practical surface for bathroom walls and floors, and continuing the same tiles over both surfaces gives an impression of space in a small room.

ABOVE RIGHT A patchwork of non-matching antique tiles makes a gorgeous surround for this basin. To produce this effect with new tiles, choose similar designs in shades of the same color and use a few of each pattern.

small lumps rather than sharp shards. Safety glass, which is reinforced by fine lines of wire running through it in a grid pattern, has also been used in some modern schemes. It has a slight blue-green cast and sometimes comes with a textured finish.

Glass is not an expensive material, but having it cut to size, finished, and erected can be costly. The glass sheets or walls need to be cut to the exact size and the edges polished or rounded off-site, then transported to their destination and assembled. When the glass is in place, the edges and seams, especially in shower enclosures, must be sealed.

Stone has good waterproof qualities and comes in many types and finishes. Marble, once found only in rich households, is now more widely and cheaply available in tiles, veneers, and marble and resin composites. The composites are lighter than the pure stone and can have a warmer, slightly softer touch. They are also easier to cut and can be premolded into a number of shapes.

THIS PAGE Glossy white, brick-shaped tiles were popular in the 1930s when their clinical look was in step with the fashion for health and hygiene. In a bathroom where the old fixtures have survived, it is worth retaining the tiles to keep the décor intact.

Shower enclosures are often made of toughened glass; this material can also be used to create surfaces around basins and splashbacks around the edges of bathtubs.

Limestone and granite both come in a choice of muted natural colors, and can be bought in tile form as well as cut to order for a splashback or sink area. The advantage of specially cut lengths is that there are no seams or gaps that need to be sealed to prevent water from seeping through.

Wood makes an attractive finish in a bathroom, but it should be chosen for its water resilience and treated to make it water-repellent. Constant contact with water can cause kiln-dried and naturally dried wood to split, and water may stain and mark an unfinished or natural surface. Although there are many paler woods available, the fashion is for dark woods. Teak is an endangered species, but rubberwood, iroko, and merbau are acceptable substitutes. Many tropical woods have inherent antibacterial and water-repellent properties. Wood soaps are useful for cleaning, or a damp cloth will remove surface buildup, but keep detergents away from woods.

ABOVE AND ABOVE LEFT Both mirror and glass complement the sleek style of a contemporary bathroom, reflecting light within the room or allowing it to enter from adjoining spaces. Rigid, smooth, seamless, and waterproof, glass performs well in a wet room, and though it shows watermarks, they are easily polished away. As a matter of safety, only thick reinforced glass is suitable for walls or partitions, and it can be transparent to give a sense of space or etched for more privacy.

LEFT AND BELOW Slate is impervious to water, but as the stone is usually applied in tiles or panels, the joints between them must be sealed to prevent moisture penetration. Slate comes with a polished, flat, or gently rippled surface, with the latter giving a less slippery surface when wet.

BOTTOM Lining the walls with the same material from which the tub or basin is made gives the bathroom a cavelike feel. Stones such as marble or limestone are suitable for this treatment.

Another popular surface for bathroom walls and cupboards is tongue-and-groove wooden paneling, which can be painted or left plain and sealed. It can be used to hide unsightly items—from uneven walls to pipework and toilet tanks. Covering the walls below dado height with tongue-and-groove will make a large room seem cozier.

Composite board can be routed to create panellike sections similar to tongue-and-groove or recessed panels. You can buy or make fancy edging strips with composite—in scalloped shapes, for example—to bring pattern and a decorative finish to a frieze, the top of a cupboard, or the edge of a bath panel. Composite in a bathroom must be well sealed and finished.

Ordinary plaster is not generally suitable for bathrooms unless it is carefully finished with a waterproof seal—otherwise, the plaster will absorb water and eventually start to powder and shale. Any cracks, even in waterproofed

RIGHT Mirror will enhance space and light, but its candid reflections can be unforgiving. The blemished surface of these distressed, antiqued mirror panels are kinder to the bather.

BELOW White painted tongue-and-groove paneling looks clean and fresh in a country bathroom.

BOTTOM Horizontal pine boards create the rustic look of a log cabin. The boards are sealed to reduce warping and the spaces between filled with white calk for a striped result.

plaster, can absorb moisture and become damaged. One plaster that can withstand the rigors of the bathroom is Armourcast, which contains a durable marble dust. Walls and surfaces to which plaster is applied should be well prepared, and the finished dry wall should be waxed, varnished, or sealed.

Sheets of steel can be lightweight and water-resistant, and molded to form a seamless basin and splashback in one. Bathtub surrounds can also be preformed. Too much steel can make a bathroom appear cold and inhospitable, so it should be mixed with natural materials and softened by using color, either on the walls or in accessories such as towels.

Most leading paint manufacturers now make lines of paint suitable for bathrooms, including flat vinyl, vinyl silk, and vinyl soft sheen. Surfaces covered with vinyl paints are easy to wipe clean with a cloth and a mild detergent. An anticondensation paint is available that reduces buildup of condensation and contains a fungicide to protect the surface against mold. This sort of paint is ideal for use around a shower enclosure with an open top where steam rises and cools, covering the wall with rivulets of moisture. Painted stencil patterns can be a good alternative to wallpaper borders and friezes that are vulnerable to peeling and damage.

Ceramic tiles have long been a standard wall covering for bathrooms. Particularly popular today are the small mosaic tiles that come in strips with removable backing. The mesh or brown paper backing is cut with a sharp knife and the unwanted section of tiles put aside for later use. Mosaic tiles can be used to create many different patterns or pictures.

If you are laying standard-sized tiles, 4 x 4in (100 x 100mm), consider making a pattern with plain tiles rather than using

For woods that lack good water tolerance, seal surfaces that will be regularly exposed to water with a polyurethane finish or yacht varnish.

ABOVE **Veneered wood panels are a sophisticated choice for bathroom walls, but in the absence of tiles, the area around the tub or basin must be finished to protect against moisture.**

LEFT **Bleached softwood paneling has a cool, chic look, but is a suitably modest backdrop for this modern country bedroom and bathroom. The light color and the horizontal boards make the room appear larger.**

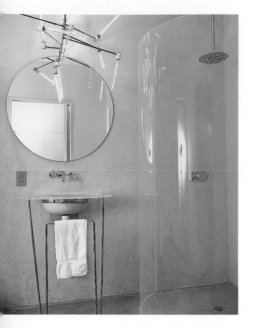

Some mosaics, like those seen on floors of ancient Roman baths, are of emperors and gods; others are simple bands of pattern.

surface-patterned or transfer-decorated tiles. For example, the square tiles can be placed on their points to form diamonds. Rectangular, brick-shaped tiles can be set in regular lines or staggered so they overlap. Mixing shapes and colors can also be interesting. A simple checkerboard effect can be produced with traditional black and white tiles, or with light and dark shades of the same color.

As an alternative to factory-made glazed ceramic tiles, there are unique—if costly—handmade and painted designs. Some of them have objects or pieces of metal pressed into them. Glass tiles are also available in a rainbow of colors.

Flat effects include encaustic tiles, where the pattern is made by inlaying contrasting colors of clay slip into the surface of the tile. This style of decoration was first used in medieval monastery flooring in Europe, but has been updated to provide innovative designs with natural, non-gloss, stonelike finishes.

ABOVE Concrete and plaster in their unrefined state have a raw integrity that suits certain modern interiors. Sealed with a clear waterproof finish, they make perfect wall finishes for the bathroom.

walls: key points

• **glass**—only laminated, toughened, or safety glass should be used in a bathroom.

• **stone**—for good waterproof qualities, the choices range from marble to slate.

• **paint**—finishes suitable for a bathroom are widely available in many colors.

THIS PAGE **In a room where the scheme is a deep, saturated blue, the flat color is relieved by the slight tonal variations and texture of mosaic. This well-groomed, perfectly regular version is made up of smooth ovals of polished ceramic. A suitable wall surface for wet areas, mosaic is much less prone to cracking or chipping than larger tiles.**

• **wood**—needs to be sealed to protect it from water. Oily hardwoods are the best choice as they are resilient to moisture.

• **tiles**—ceramic tiles are a traditional surface material, but glass tiles are currently popular.

• **steel**—lightweight and waterproof, it can be molded to form basins, bath panels, and surrounds.

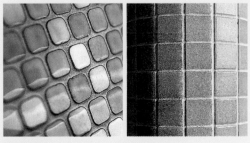

• **plaster**—must be finished with a waterproof seal.

THIS PAGE **This pattern of tiles, sometimes known as octagon and dot, has been used for centuries, often in the stone-floored hallways of old houses. Although usually found in black and white, here, cream and red-brown tiles give a modern look. Marble or limestone are the classic materials for this type of floor, but ceramic and vinyl versions are also available.**

flooring

Bathroom flooring should be durable, waterproof, and non-slip. In many simply furnished modern bathrooms, it has also become the focus of color and decoration.

Many bathrooms are small, and a single color on the floor gives an impression of space—while a heavily patterned linoleum or vinyl-tile design might be too busy and overpowering. The main problem with dark flooring in a bathroom is that it shows up dust and talcum powder, which are less visible on lighter coverings.

When choosing a floor covering, consider comfort, safety, and hygiene as well as color and pattern. Visit building supply and commercial flooring outlets

BELOW LEFT A checkered black and white floor is a key element in this mono-chromatic bathroom. Stone setts have been painted to match the overall scheme. Laying the tiles at an angle to the walls makes the room look wider.

as well as domestic retailers so that you are aware of the range of alternatives. Carpet is one option—but cork, rubber, linoleum, vinyl, and wooden flooring are preferable because they are water-repellent and simple to clean, as well as being comfortable under bare feet.

Cork, which comes from the outer bark of the cork oak, *Quercus suber*, is a good insulator against cold and noise, and has a warm, cushionlike feel underfoot; it is durable and, if sealed, resilient to wear and tear. Cork's natural color is a warm honey-brown. It can be stained or colored in many shades, but it should be sealed with a polyurethane finish. Buy cork that has already been impregnated with sealant rather than trying to apply the finish once the floor is in place. Flooring that is insufficiently sealed will swell and crack if it absorbs water from a spill or flood.

ABOVE A Greek key border and a change of background color have been used on the floor of this wet room to visually separate the shower from the bathing area. The brick walls must be an original feature, and the bathtub a vintage model, but the floor covering is recent. However, by choosing mosaic—a timeless surface in a classical design—the contrast between old and new is less marked.

LEFT **Matt gray stone gives a harder, more masculine edge to the mirrored and white painted surfaces in this bathroom. Although stone flooring may seem cold and unforgiving, a slightly textured surface can give an appearance of warmth that is lacking in glossy polished stone. Underfloor heating makes a tangible difference to the comfort of stone flooring.**

BELOW **A pale floor completes the pristine look of an all-white bathroom, but the texture of a natural material softens what could** be a clinical look. The floor is covered with highly figured plywood, which has been painted with diluted white paint and then sanded to reveal the grain of the wood. The floor is finally sealed with transparent acrylic lacquer.

RIGHT **Wood flooring is best reserved for bathrooms that are used by adults who will respect its sensitivity to water. Even then, the choice of wood is important, and closely-fitted floors like this one must be made from a hardwood with natural resistance to moisture.**

Untreated wood is vulnerable to damage by water and extremes of temperature, but wood that has been properly seasoned and sealed can provide a natural, versatile, and resilient covering for a bathroom floor.

Cork can be bought in tiles or by the roll. There are various grades of thickness—choose the sort that is suitable for floors rather than the thinner product intended for walls. Some tiles are not only impregnated with a water-repellent finish, but also have a solid rubber backing, which makes them ideal for a bathroom and increases warmth and sound insulation.

Most rubber flooring is textured with a raised pattern or ribbing, creating a non-slip surface. Available in sheet or tile form, and in a wide choice of colors and finishes, rubber is attached with a strong adhesive to a solid base.

If you want to lay rubber on an existing floor of wooden planks, you may first have to lay a subfloor of wooden sheeting or composite board so the floor surface is stable and will not cause the tiles to move and tear over seams. Rubber has

a certain amount of sound insulation; it is also water-resistant and can be cleaned thoroughly with a brush or a mop.

Linoleum is made from a combination of natural ingredients—linseed oil, finely ground wood, pine resin, and natural pigments—pressed onto a jute backing. A reasonably flexible product, it is strong, easy to clean, water-resistant, and comparatively warm underfoot.

Vinyl is a chemically manufactured covering available in many colors and patterns. As with certain linoleum products, it can be laser-cut to order to create a wide range of patterns and pictures. Vinyl comes in a variety of thicknesses and finishes; some, such as cushioned vinyl, are ideal for the bathroom because they have a soft and spongy feel underfoot.

Bare wood can be damaged by water and extremes of temperature, but if the wood is treated, seasoned, and sealed, it can provide a natural and versatile surface. Expensive hardwoods such as elm, ash, walnut, oak, and maple are best left in their natural color so that their intrinsic beauty and the pattern of the grain shows through. Cheaper softwoods such as pine can be decorated with paint washes and stains—a technique that may also be used to revive damaged or time-worn wooden floors. Pickled, stained, and painted

TOP AND ABOVE Combining floor coverings is an imaginative way of dealing with the opposing needs of different parts of the bathroom. Water-resistant materials tend to be cold, whereas warm surfaces are rarely suitable for wet areas, so here stone tiles have been laid in the shower and hardwood decking outside.

Carpet, although luxurious underfoot, is not as hardwearing in a damp environment as many other floor coverings. It is wise to lay it only in rooms that are comparatively dry and used exclusively by adults.

floors should all be finished with a water-resistant sealant such as gloss or flat varnish. For a really durable finish, choose marine varnish—used to seal the wooden decks of boats—but you may need to apply several coats to build up a waterproof seal.

Wooden floors come in a variety of shapes and styles—from planks to parquet. If you are planning to lay a new wooden floor, ask the supplier which type is best for your circumstances.

Types of hard flooring used in modern designs include concrete, slate, stone, terracotta, and ceramic tiles. Many of these finishes have traditionally been dismissed for bathroom flooring because they are cold underfoot, but this problem can now be solved by underfloor heating.

Concrete can be laid in a thin screed onto a sealed subfloor and the heating conduits laid in place and smoothed over before the concrete sets. The

TOP LEFT **Some natural floor coverings, such as coir, sisal, and wool, are not advisable for use in a bathroom where they will get very wet. But in an elegant, airy room where bathing is a relaxed affair, they will not be damaged by occasional splashes.**

ABOVE **Carpet is the most luxurious flooring, but not the most practical for a bathroom. Here, where the style of furnishing is more like a living room than a bathroom, it is entirely appropriate.**

surface of the concrete can be finished to create a smooth, slightly shiny appearance or lightly textured with a wood-grain effect or simple linear marks. Alternatively, it can be colored with dyeing agents to give a warmer and more domestic appearance.

Concrete is durable, waterproof, and easy to clean, but anything fragile that is dropped on it will almost certainly break. The plain appearance of a standard concrete floor can be broken up with mats, rugs, or sections of wooden duckboard placed on appropriate areas of the floor.

Slate has also benefited from underfloor heating, and from modern finishes that make it more resilient and less likely to shale or flake. Slate is waterproof and comes in beautiful earthy tones ranging from green and blue-gray to amber pink. The main disadvantage of a slate floor is that it can be noisy when hard objects are moved across it.

Other stone floor coverings such as granite are similarly hard and noisy, but they are also hardwearing and waterproof, and come in a whole spectrum of colors from white to black, with flecks of gold- and silver-colored metals in their seams. These surfaces perform well in a bathroom with a steam

Rubber flooring has traditionally been used for industrial coverings, but it works equally well in home bathrooms.

cabinet because they will not be adversely affected by high temperatures or a damp atmosphere.

Tiles made of materials such as terracotta and ceramic are durable, waterproof, and less expensive than those made of stone or slate. Terracotta tiles can be manufactured with a textured and handmade appearance. Ceramic tiles used on the floor should be specially made for the purpose rather than those meant for walls or work surfaces.

Mosaic is another water-resistant and decorative floor covering. Mosaics can be made from stone—even from pebbles, although pebble mosaics tend to be knobbly to walk on—and glazed, flat, or vitreous glass tiles. Laying a mosaic picture requires skill and patience. The design must be accurately assembled on the floor, in a dry state, before being set into cement.

ABOVE **Rubber tiles inject a lively shot of color into this all-white shower room. Ideal for a family bathroom that gets heavy use, rubber is waterproof, warm to the touch, resilient, and comes in a vast choice of colors. The color goes right through the tiles, so they will retain their brilliance for years.**

flooring: key points

• **practicalities**—consider safety, comfort, and hygiene as well as the visual aspects of color and pattern.

• **hard flooring**—especially practical when teamed with underfloor heating. Choices include concrete, slate, stone, terracotta, and ceramic tiles.

THIS PAGE **Sheet flooring materials like linoleum and rubber are slip-resistant, hardwearing, and easily maintained. They come in a palette of plain colors and, expertly laid, give a smooth and apparently seamless surface. Decoratively, this flat sweep of color is an effective background for a simple, modern bathroom.**

• **linoleum and vinyl**—warm underfoot, easy to clean, water-resistant, and available in a range of colors and patterns.

• **wood**—offers a natural, versatile surface but must be treated, seasoned, and sealed.

• **rubber**—usually textured to create a non-slip surface. Offering water resistance and sound insulation, it is a good bathroom flooring option.

• **cork**—hardwearing, an efficient sound absorber, and warm to the touch. It can be stained in many shades to match the color scheme of your bathroom.

ABOVE AND LEFT **A series of uplighters spaced at intervals along a border of pebbles would, in any other setting, be designed to lead the way along a path or corridor, but here, their purpose is to provide** decorative and dramatic effect. Their beams graze the surface of an old brick wall, highlighting its earthy color and robust texture in contrast to the immaculate pale stone on the opposite side of the room.

lighting

A bathroom needs two types of artificial light: the bright and lively kind that gives clear illumination, and the soft, subtle, relaxing kind. To achieve the right balance requires good planning.

If you have a window in your bathroom, put the basin near it to take advantage of daylight—which is, after all, the best and cheapest source of illumination you can have. Natural light also gives a much more realistic idea of skin tone and color than artificial light. No matter how good the natural light in your bathroom, when it comes to shaving or other tasks that involve close scrutiny, or at darker times of the day or year, it will need to be enhanced with electric lighting.

Few safety warnings can be more basic but vital in a bathroom: water and electricity are a dangerous, potentially fatal combination. Nowhere in the home do they come in closer proximity than in the bathroom. The bathroom is also a place where you are frequently vulnerable, without clothing or shoes that might ground or insulate you from a shock, and naked skin can be scorched and easily damaged. So, for your own wellbeing, heed all safety warnings relating to electrical fixtures and bathroom lights and make sure that any electrical work carried out in a bathroom is done by a professional.

When planning a lighting scheme for the bathroom, it is essential to consult a qualified electrician to make sure your proposals are safe. Any lamps or fixtures for bathroom use must be specially made for wet environments and

BELOW LEFT **A concealed fluorescent lamp sheds a downward light onto the basin without dazzling the eye. This is a specific task light, and additional lighting will be required for the mirror and, more generally, to illuminate the room.**

BELOW RIGHT **Mirror lights should illuminate the face of the person looking into it, not the mirror itself. These lights, almost the same height as the mirror, have frosted glass shades giving a soft, diffuse light for even illumination without glare. The chrome fixtures are reminiscent of Art Deco style and are in keeping with the glamorous, retro look of this bathroom.**

Task lighting, targeted over a basin, should offer a clean, even illumination for activities involving close scrutiny.

enclosed in sealed covers or shades to protect them from the effects of steam and condensation. No lighting fixture should be within reach of a person who might be seated or standing in the area of the shower or the bathtub.

Low-voltage lighting can generally be used safely as long as the bulbs are in enclosed fixtures and any sockets are double-insulated. Once the safety factors have been taken care of, you can focus on the creative business of arranging the lighting.

It may be useful to have two electrical circuits that can be operated from a panel outside the bathroom and equipped with dimmer switches. Some of these panels can be programmed so that you have only to touch a particular number for lighting that is bright, mid-level, or specifically targeted. In addition, mid-level wall lights can be used to soften and even out shadows cast by overhead lights.

Designate a central ceiling area for a functional or ambient light—an all-purpose illumination to turn on when you enter the room. It can take the form of a central ceiling light or a central row of recessed downlighters. The latter work well in a bathroom with a low ceiling because, unlike a ceiling light, they don't intrude on headroom.

In addition to functional lighting, task lighting is necessary to facilitate detailed duties such as shaving, make-up application, teeth flossing, and general maintenance. Target this on the mirror over the basin, where most

ABOVE LEFT The grid effect of the translucent partition walls dominates this bathroom so other fixtures must be kept simple. The mirror above the basin is unframed and the lamps flanking it plain chrome-capped strip lights. The light they give is crisp and white, and while it will not add to the atmosphere of the room, it gives clear, honest illumination for shaving and makeup.

ABOVE A recessed, low-voltage downlighter, producing light out of all proportion to the size of the fixture, is positioned to illuminate both the bathroom and the adjoining shower enclosure. The glass bricks forming the partition between bathroom and shower are obscured for privacy and catch the light with sparkling results, an effect enhanced by the brilliant white and stainless-steel surfaces.

RIGHT AND BELOW In a bathroom equipped with stainless-steel fixtures, a pair of custom-designed stainless-steel baffles conceal the strip lights that fit between the sides of the mirror and the recessed glass-fronted cupboards. Although the basin is small, the baffles—effectively an illuminated mirror frame—give it more importance and the combined fixtures take on the appearance of a wall-mounted vanity unit. When the lights are turned on, the basin and mirror can be seen through the tinted glass doors that separate the bathroom from the living room, but when they are off, the doors lose their transparency and the room beyond is invisible. By day, the reverse occurs, and the windowless bathroom enjoys some natural light.

> If possible, site your basin near a window to take advantage of natural light—the best and cheapest source of illumination.

activities involving close scrutiny take place. Task lighting should offer a clean, even, shadow-free illumination. This is best provided by a strip light with a tungsten or fluorescent tube, or by two well-placed and well-balanced side lights. Some mirrors have their own built-in lights, and some fluorescent-strip fixtures have integral shaving sockets.

Target lighting may also be useful where a toilet or shower is in a separate cubicle or recessed behind a wall in an area that has insufficient ambient or natural light of its own. The shower enclosure and toilet can be specifically targeted with downlighters or spotlights.

Interesting combinations of lighting with an integral secondary feature are also available for use in a bathroom. These include a light/ventilator—ideal for a powder room or small bathroom because the fan or ventilator is activated as soon as the light switch is turned on. Another variation is the light/heater, which can be very useful in small rooms where one wall is an outside wall and a small radiator is either impractical—due to lack of wall space—or inadequate. A light/heater is mounted on a wall above head height and operated by means of a pull cord.

ABOVE LEFT **A pair of wall brackets with conical shades throws a wide pool of light down over the mirror and basin in this traditional bathroom. The candle-sconce style of the lamps is in keeping with the look of the room but does not compete with the ornate mirror frame.**

ABOVE **Daylight is the main source of light in this country bathroom, and it is enhanced by the white walls and reflective cream ceiling. At night, a single recessed downlighter illuminates the tub and the picture that hangs over it, creating an atmosphere of intimacy and relaxation.**

Whatever style of bathroom you choose, there is a wide selection of bathroom light fittings to match. These range from period-inspired lights with opal glass and chrome fixtures to ceiling lights made up of several adjustable arms that can be arranged to make an interesting shape as well as to give a wide pool of light. Wall lights can be round, rectangular, square, or diamond-shaped, and you may find that an opaque finish gives a softer, more diffuse light than clear glass.

A flat disk that screws into a metal plate is not the only type of enclosed shade. There are glass orbs or globes that stand proud of the wall on backplates or adjustable brackets; angular shades that complement the angular lines of Art Deco fixtures; and flamelike glass shades with fixtures that resemble a torch. Bulkhead fixtures, modeled on those used in ships, are both watertight and have nautical overtones that can enhance the utilitarian mood of an industrially inspired chrome bathroom. Although clear or plain glass shades give the most effective light for tasks requiring close scrutiny, colored shades and tinted bulbs can add a lighthearted or decorative element to a bathroom.

ABOVE LEFT The lighting plan emphasizes the symmetrical arrangement of fixtures in this room. A series of matching pendant lamps hang high above the tub, and wall lights flank the window and illuminate a pair of arch chairs. The fixtures are simple and add to the purity of the scheme.

ABOVE RIGHT Like the antique candle sconces on which their design is based, these elegant double wall lamps have mirrored backplates to magnify the light they produce. Equipped with tungsten bulbs, they give a warm light not dissimilar to candlelight, which is flattering both to the décor and to the complexion.

Where a bathroom is not overlooked, keep the window uncovered during the day to allow as much daylight in as possible.

A level of illumination that is restful but not too dramatic can be created by using wall lights controlled by a dimmer switch. Some spa and whirlpool baths have lights below the water level so that, when they are lit, the inside of the bathtub and the swirling water become the focal point in a room where the ambient light has been dimmed. Lights recessed into a floor have thick, ribbed-glass, domed lids that screw into a metal casing. These can be used to create pools of light up walls, in corners, or beside steps leading up to a sunken bathtub.

Spotlights—ceiling-mounted or hidden behind a shelf or in an appropriate corner—can be used to highlight particular features. The level of light directed at the feature should be at a more intense level than the ambient light in the rest of the room so the feature stands out.

ABOVE **Natural light from the window and glazed interior door means that no additional illumination is needed during the day. Frosted glass in both the door and window diffuses the natural light, making it appear whiter and brighter, and the mostly white décor adds to the effect.**

lighting: key points

• **safety first**—water and electricity are dangerous partners, so it is important that you always employ a qualified electrician to carry out any electrical work in the bathroom.

• **light fixtures**—from elaborate period-style wall lamps to simple, recessed downlighters, there are fixtures to match every style of bathroom.

THIS PAGE The bathroom in an apartment high above the city streets is unlikely to be overlooked, and a functioning sash window glazed with obscured glass gives the choice of privacy or a view. The window has been left uncovered by curtains or blinds to allow daylight to flood into the room unhindered.

- **task lighting**—target this over the basin where most detailed grooming activities take place. Make sure the face of the user is illuminated, not the mirror itself.

- **ambient lighting**—soft lighting in a bathroom will create a relaxed atmosphere for bathing.

- **daylight**—make the most of any natural light you have in your bathroom.

- **spotlights**—use to highlight unusual special features, fixtures, or decorative details that add individuality to the room.

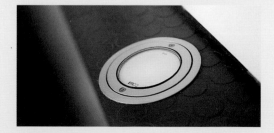

fixtures &
appliances

bathtubs and faucets, showers, basins,
toilets and bidets, heated towel rods

Bathroom fixtures are available in an ever-increasing choice of shapes, finishes, and colors, so choosing the best ones for you and your lifestyle can be difficult. When it comes to bathtubs and basins, deciding what activities they will be used for and by whom will help to determine what size and shape will best suit your needs.

bathtubs and faucets

Few things are as relaxing as a warm, scented bath. Whether you have a large, freestanding tub or a modern slimline one, soaking offers simple indulgence that can be appreciated any time of the day.

BELOW **This telephone bath/shower faucet—so-called because the hand set rests in a cradle at the top like the receiver of an old-fashioned telephone—is a common sight in traditional schemes.**

In ancient times bathtubs were made from many different natural materials, including stone and wood. The Victorians favored heavy cast iron with a glazed enameled finish on the inside of their freestanding tubs. The acrylic bathtub—a 1970s discovery that was lightweight, easy to move, and simple to plumb—gave rise to a whole range of new designs because it could be easily molded and colored.

The advent of acrylic-based materials has had a lasting effect on the landscape of the bathroom. Modern man-made substances have allowed designers to produce sleek and contemporary—yet hugely practical—fixtures and surfaces. For example, Corian ®, made by DuPont—a mixture of acrylic resin and natural minerals—is a nonporous material that can be carved into a multitude of shapes and is perfect for shower trays, and integral basins and surfaces.

RIGHT **As an alternative to a bateau or rolltop tub, an impressive freestanding bath has been created by building a custommade wooden case for an oval bathtub and edging it with a wide marble rim. Details like the curved paneling and the plinth at the base, painted to resemble stone, elevate the bathtub to luxury status.**

Since the 1990s other mixes of synthetic and natural materials have been developed, creating hybrid surfaces that are warm and light but strong and durable. Quaryl by Ucosan is made from a fusion of acrylic and quartz stone. The product is fully recyclable, has in-built noise reduction properties, and is resistant to knocks and scratches. Like Corian, Quaryl can be cut and molded into numerous shapes and forms.

Some people love the weight and solidness of a classic cast-iron bathtub, no matter whether it is an original or a reproduction. Genuine old tubs may need some work to restore them to their former glory. The cheapest option is to do this yourself with an enameling kit, but this is only suitable for covering over a small chip or crack. If a full-scale respray is required, there are companies who can send workers to your home to do the job for you or, for a more permanent and professional finish, the bathtub can be reconditioned at a workshop or factory.

FAR LEFT This rolltop tub has the faucets at one end and a sloping back rest at the other so the bather can lie back and contemplate the classical plaster plaque on the wall above. Painted a pale shade of gray, the tub's exterior tones with the quiet color scheme.

LEFT A double-ended rolltop tub has the faucets and drain set in the middle so the bather can sit at either end—or two can share a bath. This tub is painted with a border and central flourish—an idea that is easy to copy with masking tape and a stencil.

BELOW Bath mixer faucets can take many forms. The telephone mixer, far left, is wall-mounted to avoid drilling holes in the rim of the tub. A thermostatic mixer, center, has handles for hot and cold water, a dial to control temperature, a diverter, and a hand spray. Four handles, right, control the flow and temperature of the water for the bathtub and shower separately.

ABOVE Following a period format but unquestionably modern, the pared-down design of this bath/shower faucet works well in a minimal bathroom.

TOP RIGHT AND DETAIL It is unusual, but extremely practical, to place the bath spout and the shower at opposite ends of the tub. The bath can be topped up at the foot end while the shower is conveniently at hand at the head end. The faucet and shower are also controlled independently.

CENTER RIGHT To leave the rim uncluttered by a faucet, a floor-standing spout arches over the tub.

RIGHT A simple, arched spout rising from the floor and controlled by handles placed separately on the wall provides an elegant solution to delivering water to a freestanding bathtub. Plumbing for the drain is hidden by the chunky supports cradling the tub.

Modern materials for bathtubs include natural substances, such as stone and wood, as well as more streamlined stainless steel and glass.

Many modern-style bathtubs use other materials, some returning to the inspiration of the ancient Romans and the Japanese, with tubs of stone or wood. Stainless steel and reinforced glass are also popular because of their contemporary streamlined appearance.

Modern designers, such as Philippe Starck, have taken inspiration from period-style bathtubs, such as the freestanding rolltop, but have removed the claw feet and given their designs a contemporary twist. Modern versions can be set into a raised plinth to appear sunken, or placed against a wall and enclosed with panels.

Another old-fashioned classic bathtub that can be found in reproduction is the slipper tub. Smaller than other period-style tubs, it curves up at one end to facilitate bathing in a semi-sitting position.

Standard bathtubs are generally single- or double-ended and come with an apron or side panel to conceal the pipes and plumbing. Alternatively, a panel can be custom-made for your bathroom from tongue-and-groove, wood, or whatever material suits your scheme.

Bathtubs designed to cope with over-bath showers have a wider end to allow more room for movement and a shower curtain or glass panel to contain the spray. Short and small bathtubs with tapered sides have been specifically designed for small spaces, and there are also extra-large and extra-deep versions available for luxurious soaking in a big bathroom.

ABOVE LEFT **Spa baths require controls to operate the whirlpool system as well as faucets to fill the tub. Here, the controls for the spa action are ranged along the rim of the tub and those for the bath/shower mixer are set separately on the edge.**

ABOVE **A three-hole bathtub faucet often looks neater and less bulky than a mixer that combines the spout and controls in one unit. This wall-mounted faucet reinforces the uncluttered effect by leaving the rim clear.**

There are no rules about pairing traditional faucets with a classic bathtub or contemporary ones with a modern tub, but in general the simpler the combination of styles, the better the result.

Faucet designs are as wide-ranging as the tubs they serve. Choose a shape that feels comfortable in your hand and a color that complements the rest of the metalwork in your bathroom. There are no rules about pairing traditional faucets with a classic bathtub or modern ones with a contemporary version, but in general the simpler the combination of styles, the better.

Traditional designs include crossbar faucets, usually available in chrome or brass, often with ceramic disks with the words "hot" and "cold." Ceramic-covered lever faucets have a similarly old-fashioned appeal. Although modern copies of traditional faucets may look old-fashioned, they incorporate the latest technology that makes the fixture more responsive to your touch.

Faucets can be set into the rim of the tub, either at one end or halfway down its length to give a double-ended tub. Spouts can also be floor-standing or wall-mounted to give the bathtub a sleek, unencumbered look.

ABOVE **Most modern faucets are small and minimal, but these handles make a bold statement. They have studs around the barrel that make them easy to grip, and their generous size is in proportion to the large tub.**

RIGHT **Smooth curves balance the overall angular style of the room. The bathtub is rounded at both ends, the swan-neck spout clears the edge in a silvery arc, and the chrome disks on which the faucet handles rest repeat the rounded motif.**

bathtubs: key points

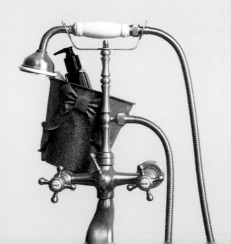

• **freestanding or boxed in?** start by identifying your ideal style of bathtub and what would work in the space you have.

• **the bathtub** is often selected as the prominent feature of the bathroom. If this is the case, keep the other fixtures simple.

• **the floor** beneath the bathtub must be solid, firm, and strong enough to hold a full tub of water.

- **slimline tubs** are made to fit small spaces, so you don't have to forego a tub if you have a small bathroom.

- **materials** used for making bathtubs come in a wide selection. Some are more high-maintenance than others, so consider your choice carefully.

- **hand-held sprays** fitted to the faucet fixture are useful for quick rinsing.

- **faucets** can be set on the rim of the bath, be wall-mounted or floor-standing, and come in a variety of styles. Choose fixtures that work best with the design of your tub.

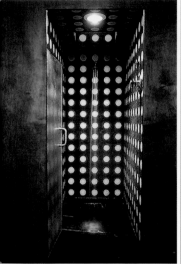

showers

Showers are refreshing and exhilarating as well as cleansing. It is believed in Asia Pacific that the fast-flowing water falling over your body enhances Ch'i, or positive energy.

ABOVE This shower area appears to be lit by shafts of bright light entering through holes in the rear wall. In reality, it is lined with dark, waterproof concrete and inlaid with light-colored tiles that glint in the overhead light.

ABOVE RIGHT A curve of frosted glass screens an otherwise open shower area from the adjoining room but allows light to pass through. A pair of ceiling-mounted sprays and a hand-held fixture offer an invigorating shower.

FAR RIGHT Built like an indoor folly, this classical temple shows how a shower cubicle can be turned into an architectural feature. Despite its amazing appearance, the structure is extremely space efficient, with cupboards at the sides and the front.

Showers were traditionally installed as an integral part of a bathtub, with the tub doubling as a shower pan. The trend is now for the two fixtures to be seen as separate items, each offering different benefits. The vogue began as a consequence of the growing popularity of whirlpool baths, when people decided they didn't want to close in their stylish tubs with curtains or doors.

In the search for ever-greater luxury, more and more elaborate super showers—characterized by multiple shower heads and finely adjustable sprays—have become widely available, with manufacturers never short of ideas for adding exciting new features. For example, it is now possible to buy super showers with built-in TV monitors and stereo/CD players, as well as electronically controlled body sprays. Most popular of all are steam units— desired for their health-promoting qualities as well as the pleasure they bring.

Technological developments such as pressure-balancing valves, which regulate water temperature and rate of flow, have brought an added degree of safety to the shower. This is particularly advantageous in a household with children. Ideally, it should be possible to turn the water on and off, and to regulate the temperature, from outside the shower cubicle.

If you do not want to embark on a complete remodel, there are various ways of adding luxury to your shower without expensive building work. One of these is to replace a single valve with a shower panel that includes multiple shower heads and body sprays.

There is a wide selection of shower enclosures to choose from. A two-sided shower enclosure, a custom-built shower cubicle, and a freestanding shower cubicle are among those available for a good-sized bathroom. The shower enclosure is a door with one or two side panels; the remaining side or sides of the enclosure are generally the existing wall or walls of the room, which have been waterproofed and tiled. The paneled sides are usually made of safety glass—one of them is rigid, the other contains the door.

BELOW This self-contained shower enclosure stands independently within an open-plan living space. The shower and its plumbing are contained in a tower fixture that stands away from the wall to prevent it from throwing a dark shadow against the glass.

BOTTOM In this wet room a double shower has been made by fitting one either side of a pillar. With separate water supplies, the showers can be used independently.

RIGHT A combination of a fixed shower head and a hand-held spray broadens the showering options. The fixed shower head can be angled to suit users of differing height, and the hand-held spray can be set at a lower level to give a dual-spray shower.

TOP A shower head and hand-held spray at different levels allow the user to wash standing up or seated on the built-in bench.

ABOVE A hand-held shower and directable body jets aimed at different levels give a head-to-toe shower.

A shower is an ideal way to start the morning, a blast of water from head to toe washing away sleepiness and preparing the mind and body for the day.

A custom-built shower cubicle is similar to an enclosure but does not depend on the pre-existence of two right-angled walls. The cubicle can be built to fit into any space. It needs a single wall, probably a long back wall, and lightweight, non-loadbearing walls, known as stud walls, can be built to create the ends.

The third option is the freestanding cubicle, which has a shower pan, walls, and roof in one molded pod that can be put almost anywhere because it does not need to be against a wall. This type of unit is appropriate in a connecting bathroom or where a shower needs to be installed quickly. It is prefabricated and can be easily put in, and there is no assembly, tiling, grouting, or sealing to be done. The modules tend to be practical, but not very stylish.

At the other end of the spectrum are spacious freestanding cubicles that come with built-in steam-sauna function, electric lights, and aromatic herb dispenser. They may also have an integrally molded seat, a programmable electronic up-and-down device that allows you to place the water jets where you want them, or thermostatic mixers to preset the temperature.

If you want to economize or prefer taking a bath to having a shower, consider an over-the-tub shower with a curtain and pole. You can hang the curtain using an L-shaped pole, which attaches to the wall at one end of the long side of the tub and then across the short side, or use a circular pole hung from the ceiling so it surrounds the area around the shower head.

An alternative to a shower curtain is a screen of reinforced safety glass that fits along part of the long open side of a tub. Although not totally spray-proof, it is about 75 percent effective. A more reliable choice is a folding bath screen, which resembles a standard screen but has an extra panel that slides out beside the fixed one. Sliding panels that fit along the entire length of the bathtub make the ultimate over-bath shower enclosure.

Shower pans come in various shapes and materials including cast iron, steel, stone, composite, and enameled fireclay. Unpolished stone has its own nonslip surface, but enameled and other shiny-surface pans need a nonslip finish. Most pans have a raised pattern, whose ridges provide a nonslip grip; or you can add a rubber mat or a wooden duckboard.

There is no standard height for a shower head. In general, the shower head should be installed at a height that suits you—perhaps 6in (15cm) above the top of your head—but it is worth discussing the options with your plumber. If

BELOW A single-control thermostatic mixer valve has one knob that controls the water temperature.

BOTTOM LEFT A traditional shower rose is teamed with an adjustable shower head that can produce either a vigorous massage spray or a soft, aerated drench.

BOTTOM CENTER Surface-run pipework can be left exposed as part of a decorative scheme.

BOTTOM RIGHT A dual-control thermostatic shower mixer has one knob for temperature and one to control the rate of flow.

In addition to boosting your vitality, showers cleanse, washing away dead skin and sweat which, if you have a bath, stays in the water with you.

TOP **A shower head with tiny projections directs water in fine jets giving a tingling sensation.**
ABOVE **An efficient central drain is essential in a wet room.**

the shower is intended for family use, it may be preferable to choose an adjustable head that can be moved up and down on a pole mounted on the wall to suit the various heights of different members of the family.

A wet room is a shower in a room that has been totally waterproofed. Well established in Europe, the wet room usually consists of a totally tiled enclosed space with a sloping floor and a central drain. Wet rooms should be professionally installed because it may be necessary to line all the surfaces with a plastic membrane to prevent leakage. A drain must be sunk into the floor, which needs to slope slightly so the water is channeled into the outflow. The shower head can be plumbed in through the wall with a simple dial or faucet beneath so there is minimal gadgetry on show.

showers: key points

- **water flow**—before installing a shower, find out what type of water supply you have and whether you need a pump.

- **enclosures**—a two-sided enclosure, a purpose-built shower cabinet, and a freestanding shower cubicle are among the options for a good-sized bathroom.

THIS PAGE **Matt surfaces prevail in this shower enclosure where the large tiles on the side walls and the mosaic at the back are all made from porcelain with a pleasing eggshell finish. The floor is covered in the same material. The soft, off-white porcelain contrasts sharply with a shower that has been antiqued with a tarnished, almost black finish. The shower fixtures are otherwise very simple with a flat disk thermostatic mixer operated by a white china handle and a traditional wall-mounted shower rose.**

• **screens**—safety-glass panels or curtains can be used to screen over-tub showers.

• **trays**—standard shower trays are square, but corner shapes and oblongs can also be found; materials include steel and stone.

• **controls**—traditional crosshead faucets, bath/shower mixer faucets, and concealed devices operated by disks or levers are popular options for shower controls.

• **heads**—shower heads can be fixed or flexible; adjustable heads offer a choice of sprays that includes intermediate, full-force, and concentrated needle spray.

basins and faucets

The size and shape of your basin should be chosen according to how often it is used and what activities it is used for. A powder room basin used only for washing hands, for example, does not need to be very big.

ABOVE **A double basin saves time for a couple in the early morning rush, but few are as magnificent as this original 1930s pedestal basin. The bridge faucets taps are also original. Such fixtures can be found in architectural salvage yards, but good reproductions are also available.**

Basins come in various sizes and shapes, and can be wall-hung, placed on a pedestal, or set into a vanity unit. When deciding on the size and shape of your basin, consider how often you use it and what activities you use it for. If the basin is in a powder room and used only for washing your hands, it does not have to be very big. Deep basins are necessary only if you need a substantial volume of water—for shaving, for example, or if children use the basin, in which case the deeper it is the better to avoid splashes.

Many basins come with a pedestal. This not only provides support for the bowl, it can also be used to disguise the pipework, which can be run down behind the recess in the back. The disadvantage of a pedestal is that it offers little choice about the height at which the basin is installed.

Wall-mounted basins can be plumbed in at a height to suit you, but the piping will need to be led out behind the basin in a special covering. Because of their streamlined appearance, wall-mounted styles are often the basin of choice in contemporary bathrooms. Corner basins do not usually come with pedestals because they are usually set on brackets that are anchored to the two long sides of the basin structure and secured to the walls on both sides.

Some basins are semi-inset into a surround, with the back part slotted into a shelf or cupboard and the front section standing away. The space around the basin is used for a soap dish or bathroom products.

An alternative is the fully inset sink, in which the bowl is set wholly into a surface, often of marble or glass. Some inset sinks are edged with a lip or rim that sits on top of the surface. Others have an unglazed rim that sits directly under the opening.

A fashionable option for a basin is the bowl and washtable effect—what appears to be a freestanding separate bowl resting on a table or glass shelf.

BELOW Victorian bathroom fixtures were sometimes embellished with transfers before being glazed. Floral designs were common.

BELOW LEFT Original Victorian and Edwardian basins tend to be larger than their modern equivalents, and designs can be flamboyant or elegant and restrained.

BOTTOM Original plumbing includes ingenious devices for operating the drain and overflow, and adds a quirky touch to a bathroom.

A round glass bowl or a rectangular ceramic one? Whatever you choose, the material and design of the basin should be in keeping with the overall style of the bathroom you are trying to create.

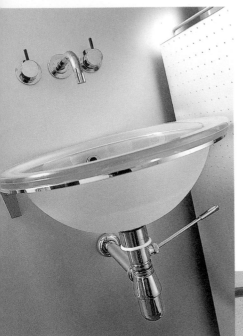

This clean and simple look is reminiscent of the traditional bowl and pitcher used in homes before built-in plumbing was invented. The modern bowl has a central drain outlet, and the faucet—usually a single sculptural monobloc and lever—is plumbed to the back, with the spout over the edge of the bowl.

Another modern development is the freestanding basin built into a frame on long legs that incorporates towel rods, soap and toothbrush holders, a shelf and mirror. It also has a faintly period look that can be traced back to the Victorian washstand combined with a gentleman's valet stand. The Washington basin is a contemporary design that consists of two concentric

ABOVE **A frosted or colored glass basin held in a wall-mounted ring bracket looks very neat, but is most suitable for a cloakroom where space is limited. If it were used in a bathroom, a cabinet, shelf, or trolley would be needed to hold toiletries.**

RIGHT **A contemporary interpretation of the old-fashioned bowl and wash stand, a ceramic basin stands on a wide stone shelf and is filled by wall-mounted faucets. The shelf is a convenient place to put toiletries, but as the style is essentially minimalist, the surface should be left bare when it is not in use.**

stainless-steel spheres. The outer bowl with the drain outlet is fixed, but the inner bowl, which pivots, holds the water while it is in use. When washing is completed, the inner bowl is tipped so the water can run out through the drain in the fixed underbowl.

Glass basins are another fashionable feature most often seen in architect-designed homes. These basins look spectacular, but they are expensive and some have to be individually made. Also, being a fashion statement, they may date quickly.

For a period-style basin you may want the most traditional sort of faucet—the pillar. Usually found in pairs, each faucet has a knob on top for turning the water on and off and individual spouts for the water to flow through. The pillar faucet can also be used in a three-hole basin mixer, in which there are separate hot and cold turning functions but no individual spouts—the water flows through a central spout. An alternative is the monobloc mixer, which consists of a central spout with integral hot and cold faucet knobs attached on either side and a lever at the back to operate the drain outlet.

ABOVE LEFT **This custom-made glass basin is long enough for two people to wash at the same time. Formed like a shelf, the basin is designed for washing under running water and has no division or plug to stop the drain.**

TOP **Midway between a wall-mounted and countertop bowl, a semi-recessed basin is set into a shelf so the plumbing is hidden behind a false wall but the front of the bowl projects into the room.**

ABOVE RIGHT **Another custommade basin, this one is made from stainless steel for a functional room. The faucets are also practical and can be operated with the wrist or elbow.**

Combining old-fashioned styles with modern technology, faucets and spouts are made to replicate those used in Victorian times but without the problems of leaking washers.

As an alternative to traditional chrome and brass finishes, you can give a classic faucet a more contemporary look with a flat finish such as satin nickel. Standard appliances such as a pillar faucet with a solid knob that is wider at the top and tapers down also combines elements of classic and modern styles.

Philippe Starck has designed some curved lever faucets that taper slightly at the top and bottom, which gives them an almost featherlike appearance. In his Starck line, the design is further simplified so a single lever and a mono mixer spout with lever-operated drain outlet form a single sculptural pillar.

The shape of modern spouts has become smoother and more rounded so that they arc over the basin. Some of the levers are sleekly slimline, resembling a fine metal rod with small, rounded, buttonlike ends for easier grip.

ABOVE **Supataps, invented in the mid-20th century, have an integrated handle and spout. Economical and functional, they are now valued for their retro charm.**

basins and faucets: key points

• **a basin** should be chosen to reflect the activities it will be used for; it needn't be very deep if used only for washing hands.

• **faucets** come in all sorts of shapes and sizes. Do you want a single spout or two— one for hot water and one for cold?

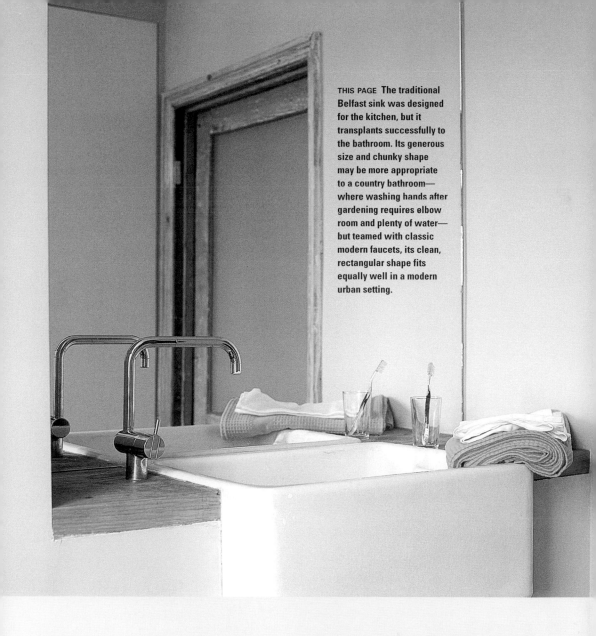

THIS PAGE The traditional Belfast sink was designed for the kitchen, but it transplants successfully to the bathroom. Its generous size and chunky shape may be more appropriate to a country bathroom— where washing hands after gardening requires elbow room and plenty of water— but teamed with classic modern faucets, its clean, rectangular shape fits equally well in a modern urban setting.

• **materials** used for making basins are numerous, with some being more practical and easier to maintain than others.

• **storage** can be added to a bathroom by choosing a basin that can be inset into a vanity unit.

• **wall-mounted basins** will give an uncluttered look and are easier to clean than pedestal versions.

• **toiletries** need to be stored somewhere. Do you want to install a shelf, a bathroom cabinet, or invest in a basin with a large enough rim to hold the essentials?

LEFT A valve-operated flush is very efficient but does not have the approval of water authorities in every country. Another way to have no visible tank is to fit an extraslim one and hide it behind a false wall.

toilets and bidets

The large majority of toilets and bidets are made from glazed ceramic whose smooth, glasslike finish looks sleek and clean and is able to withstand strong disinfectant cleaners.

The old-fashioned style of toilet had a raised tank with a bowl at the end of the metal flush pipe. The overhead tank is flushed by means of a chain and handle. These toilets fit well into a traditional bathroom, but take up wall space and are difficult to clean thoroughly because there are so many parts.

The close-coupled toilet is probably the most common style, with the tank attached to the bowl by means of a wide trunk. This is a practical, no-nonsense style of toilet, but it can take a long time

ABOVE A slipper bidet is an attractive and practical addition to a traditional bathroom. Its rounded rim and hourglass shape make it comfortable to use, while traditional crosshead faucets add to its appeal.

LEFT Victorian toilets were extremely decorative. Some of these beautifully embossed bowls still survive and look best installed with their original accessories—a dark wood seat and a high-level tank.

to clean because there are three visible parts: the tank, the join, and the bowl. In the least obtrusive type of toilet—which is uncommon in the USA—the bowl is attached directly to the wall, and the tank, generally a plastic one, is concealed behind a false wall. The tank has to be at least 32in (800mm) above the floor to provide a satisfactory flush, and the bowl is usually wall-hung, though there are some designs that come with a foot or pedestal.

Most common designs of toilet seat are made from molded plastic in a choice of solid colors. Turn-of-the-century-style bathrooms usually had wooden toilet seats, and these can also be found in modern bathrooms. Wood not only looks more attractive than plastic, but also has the advantage of feeling warmer and more comfortable to sit on. However, the wood should be well sealed so it can be cleaned occasionally with a mild detergent.

A much underrated piece of bathroom equipment, the bidet has long been part of the standard bathroom in continental Europe, but it has been slower to become established in the USA. The bidet offers benefits in terms of personal hygiene and comfort. Bidets can be either floor-standing or wall-hung. Faucets are usually the monobloc variety with a pop-up drain, and the spout is normally shorter than that found in a basin. Bidet faucets are sometimes equipped with a directional spray nozzle.

ABOVE **A modern classic, this close-coupled toilet designed by Philippe Starck has an ultraslim tank, making it a good choice for a small room.**

BELOW LEFT **The wall-mounted version of the Philippe Starck toilet gives the bathroom a clean and spacious look.**

BELOW RIGHT **Although they conform to the conventional shape, this toilet and matching bidet have a smooth, uncluttered profile that immediately identifies them as contemporary.**

heated towel rods

Specially designed heated towel rods are not generally powerful enough to provide adequate heat in a bathroom, but they have the effect of topping up the ambient heat supplied by other forms of heating.

Most heated towel rods obtain their warmth from a central-heating or hot-water system. Some are heated electrically, but they tend to be less efficient than the other types available.

The most popular type of heated towel rod is the traditional ladder-style rod finished in chrome, nickel, or gold effect. The ladder rod is often available in the form of a simple freestanding design or as a wall-mounted version.

Another option, based on the ladder style, is a double-sided rod with an arched top and two sides of rods, back and front. The double rod provides more space for spreading out towels and for the air to circulate around them to promote drying. An alternative to the arch top is the square top, which allows the towels to be fanned out over the lower rods. Simple modern heated rods follow the ladder-style design, but whereas the predominant joints are a feature of the old style, the modern version is a smooth, seamless shape.

BELOW LEFT **This custom-made towel rod, with pairs of hangers that pivot between each rung of the heated frame, has a much higher capacity than most. Because the towels do not cover the bars, they can be dried without blocking any heat.**

BELOW **This efficient ladder-type towel radiator warms the bathroom as it dries the towels. The rungs are usually arranged in groups to allow wider spaces through which larger towels can be hung.**

LEFT Heated towel rods can be mounted at virtually any height, which makes them well suited to small or built-in bathrooms where wall space at lower levels may be limited. This one is situated close to the bathtub, providing warmth where it is most needed.

A simple angular S-shaped rod is also available which provides three horizontal bars for towels.

A narrow three-bar vertical heated towel rod can be used in small spaces. This type of fixture is ideal in a gap between the basin and toilet—a space too tight for a conventional horizontal radiator. What this style of heater lacks in width, it makes up for in height, and the overall area emitting heat is comparable to that of the horizontal version.

The concept of the designer towel rod has grown out of the development of the radiator. No longer purely functional appliances, towel rods are now designed in a range of interesting shapes, from crossover X styles to bow-fronted arcs. They are also available in a choice of colors.

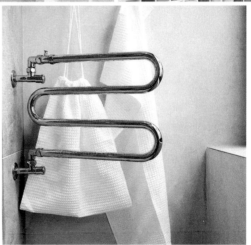

TOP RIGHT Heated towel rods come in many shapes, sizes, and colors. The rods can be round, or flattened in cross section and straight, or bow-fronted. Finishes can be metallic, solid, or colored to order.

ABOVE A Cobra-Therm towel rod is a heated tube formed in a series of serpentine curves. It may be mounted permanently against the wall or, as shown here, equipped with a useful swivel device.

fixtures and appliances notes

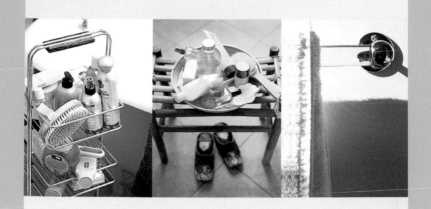

storage,
furniture, &
accessories

cupboards and vanity units, freestanding
storage and furniture, racks and mirrors

Bathroom storage is essential for making day-to-day items accessible when they are needed and for keeping the room free from clutter. Furniture not only adds a homey touch, it can also provide useful storage space or a comfortable place to sit. Accessories provide the final touches to the room and help give it a cohesive feel.

THIS PAGE **The most flexible storage of all is a freestanding cabinet and, with castors instead of feet, this one can be easily moved around. Built to the same format as a bedside table, it has a drawer to hold small items and a cupboard for larger things like cleaning products. The bright stainless-steel finish is resistant to steam, easy to clean, and looks good in a contemporary bathroom.**

storage

A neat bathroom is more conducive to relaxing, bathing, and grooming than one that is littered with half-used shampoo bottles and damp towels. Good storage will bring the clutter under control.

Built-in cupboards and vanity units generally provide bathroom storage, but there are situations where freestanding cabinets, rods, racks, and containers are a useful addition or a practical alternative. As with all bathroom storage, the freestanding kind should combine open shelves or glazed cabinets for display and closed storage for those items you would prefer to hide.

In bathrooms where space or budget is limited, the traditional bathroom cabinet mounted on the wall above the basin provides basic storage for essentials. In its simplest form, the bathroom cabinet is a rectangular cupboard with a mirrored front and shelves inside, but more elaborate versions incorporate a light and an electric razor outlet.

Floor-standing cabinets, trolleys, and shelf units are a useful addition to most bathrooms and occupy varying amounts of floor space. Cabinets are generally low and square with a cupboard, drawers, or a combination of the two. Some have castors to allow them to be moved easily for cleaning. Storage trolleys are designed for maneuverability and may have brakes so they can be parked wherever they are needed. These mobile units range in style from mesh or polished metal trolleys to contemporary wood designs and rustic painted cupboards.

Freestanding shelf units are efficient space savers, condensing the maximum of storage into the minimum of floor space. Available in various widths, they can make use of difficult spaces. Like cabinets, shelves come in many materials. Glass shelves must be made from special toughened glass and have polished edges. They are ideal for small spaces as they allow light to pass through. Glass is impervious to cleaning products and cosmetics, and

ABOVE **A portable two-tier basket is useful for moving toiletries from the bathtub to the basin or shower. Made from sturdy metal mesh, its contents are always visible.**

BELOW LEFT **A walk-in closet reduces the amount of storage needed in the bathroom, as it can store towels and other bulky essentials as well as the clothing and bedlinen it was designed to hold.**

BELOW **Here, a display case has been made by dividing an alcove to form pigeon holes with a clear plastic box to hold the contents—in this case, a stunning collection of fossils and crystals.**

Storage is especially important in a streamlined bathroom, where the aim is a clutter-free space. There are also safety reasons for keeping the room neat—it reduces the danger of tripping on objects left around.

is easy to wipe clean. Painted shelves are practical and easy to refresh with a new coat of paint when they begin to look shabby. Wire mesh is well suited for shelves, but the mesh will not contain spilt liquids. Wood shelves intended for bathroom use will be protected with a durable finish, but furniture designed for other rooms may not be so resistant to bathroom products.

Even in the smallest bathroom, space can be found to hang wall shelves. Ready-made units are simply screwed to the wall but cut-to-size shelves will fit any available space. Shelves built into an alcove or recess give a neat finish and, if they are made from glass, look stunning if lit from above.

Towel rods keep towels neat and allow them to air after use. Unheated towel rods are generally made from wood, plastic, or metal, and can be wall-mounted or floor-standing. The wall-mounted types take the form of a ring or a

ABOVE LEFT By keeping items on shelves instead of in cupboards, they are less likely to get mislaid. The disadvantage of this is that things will get dusty, but glass jars and clear plastic boxes will help keep them clean while allowing them to be seen.

ABOVE RIGHT Toiletries and clothing are stored close together in this dressing room. The extensive shoe collection is arranged in an orderly fashion in cubbyholes and smaller items are sorted in baskets.

single or double straight rod supported on brackets in a design to match other wall-mounted accessories in the bathroom. Towel rings are intended to hold a hand towel and are placed alongside a basin or bidet, but straight rods are large enough to hold a bath towel. Floor-standing rods usually have more than one rail and allow several towels to hang at once. A recent variation on the floor-standing rod is the towel ladder—a wide, straight ladder made from wood or metal that leans against the wall with the towels hung over its rungs.

Racks that keep the things you need on hand are essential in the bathtub and shower area. Individual wall-mounted holders for soaps, sponges, shaving equipment, toothbrushes, and toilet paper can be put where they are needed. In the shower, corner shelves and tiered sets of wire baskets hold shampoos and shower gel within easy reach. Most wall-mounted racks and holders are screwed to the wall, but in areas with tiled or glass walls, fixtures that are attached by suction pads are easier to install.

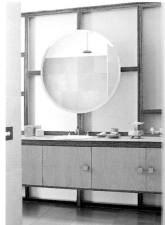

BELOW **A vanity unit presents a neat appearance in a modern bathroom, with cupboards large enough to provide all kinds of bathroom storage.**

THIS PAGE **This double vanity unit containing twin basins is built to fill a whole wall on one side of the bathroom. Storage is divided between cupboards and drawers with a pull-out hamper for laundry.**

A laundry basket is essential in any bathroom to take used towels and discarded dirty clothes. A hamper with a lid looks neat, but it should be ventilated to prevent damp towels from becoming musty.

Bath racks that rest like a bridge across the tub hold all the necessary equipment for bathing, and some luxurious models have integral book rests, candle holders, or a shaving mirror. Those who like greater freedom of movement when bathing may prefer the smaller soap and sponge racks that hook over one side of the tub.

A laundry basket helps to keep the bathroom neat. Towels and clothes can be dropped into it the moment they are discarded. Some laundry hampers are lined with a fabric bag that can be detached, allowing the laundry to be carried straight to the washing machine. Choose one that is large enough for your needs. A family that puts muddy sports items, children's dirty clothes, and damp towels in the laundry hamper will need one that is easily washed or wiped clean, while a laundry basket that holds dry, relatively clean clothes can afford to be less robust.

ABOVE **Resourceful salvage hunters can often find items that can be reused in the home. This wire mesh sorting rack rescued from a mail room has been transformed into an ideal compartmentalized shelf for the bathroom.**

storage: key points

• **how much storage do you need?** Could bulky items, such as towels, be stored in a dressing room or linen cupboard instead?

• **wall-mounted cupboards**, cabinets, and shelves are great for smaller bathrooms because they appear to take up less space than if they were floor-standing.

THIS PAGE Sometimes the most obvious forms of storage are easily forgotten and no bathroom should be without robe hooks or a laundry basket. Put hooks on the back of the door or, as here, on a sliver of wall that otherwise would be unused. In a family bathroom, pegs fixed at a low level encourage children to be neat.

• **freestanding units** that can be easily moved around the room make cleaning less of a chore.

• **auctions and salvage yards** are great places to find unusual storage items that can be transplanted into your bathroom.

• **laundry hampers** are made from plastic, wire, metal, wicker, or wood, and some are simple fabric bags that hang from wooden or metal frames. Choose a style that matches your overall scheme.

accessories

A streamlined bathroom should have the minimum of accessories. In the indulgent bathroom, a few more objects may be on show, but not so many that the room appears cluttered and messy.

ABOVE AND RIGHT
Accessories that highlight the style of the room are valuable in both decorative and practical terms. Here, an elaborate inlaid and engraved mirror and some alabaster containers add to the exotic style of the room.

LEFT The simplest designs are often the most effective, and this soap rack—a very basic construction of narrowly spaced chrome bars angled toward the center—lets soap drain.

ABOVE Everyday materials can be used to make uniquely attractive bathroom accessories like this decorative wirework holder. Hung on a nail hammered into the bathroom wall, it lets soap and sponges drip dry over the bathtub.

Oils and other bath preparations may be left on show in the bathroom, but for display it is a good idea to decant them into matching bottles or containers that have a similar appearance to give the room a more cohesive look. The containers should also coordinate with jars or boxes in which you keep dry cosmetic aids such as cotton balls and cotton swabs.

Many of the beautiful handmade soaps on the market are made with natural organic products such as oatmeal or herbs, which are sometimes suspended within a translucent bar. A few bars can be arranged in a bowl and set on a shelf or windowsill to make an attractive decorative feature.

Other washing accessories include loofahs, natural sponges, pumice stones, and body brushes to stimulate the circulation and remove dead skin cells. These natural products not only do their job extremely well, but they also look attractive and can be arranged to dry on a decorative dish.

Mirrors are an essential part of a bathroom, not only because they enable you to see yourself during the rituals of teeth-cleaning, shaving, and applying make-up, but also because they reflect light and make the room seem more airy and spacious than it is. Among the most useful are no-mist mirrors, which do not steam up—you can choose between those with a specially treated surface and those that are backed with a wafer-thin heating pad.

A bathroom may need two types of mirror: an ordinary one for general maintenance and a magnifying one for activities that involve close scrutiny.

BELOW LEFT **A rack that spans the width of the tub holds everything close at hand. Bath racks can be made from plastic, wood, or metal with a chrome or gold finish.**

BELOW RIGHT **A wicker hamper provides extra bathroom storage when there is no scope for adding more shelves or cabinets. Because the space inside it is not divided, it will hold bulky objects like babies' bath toys, spare towels, or toilet-paper rolls, but it can be easily adapted for smaller items by putting them in plastic containers.**

Small accessories such as toothbrush holders should be chosen to complement the bathroom scheme to give the design a cohesive feel.

TOP **Set in the corner of a shower enclosure, a wall-mounted wire tray will hold toiletries within easy reach. Its open framework allows water to run through.**

ABOVE **Unbreakable containers are the safest option in a room where bottles can slip through wet, soapy hands. Chrome versions look stylish and won't break if dropped.**

RIGHT **Wall-mounted racks and shelves help to keep the basin area clear of accessories and avoid a cluttered look.**

There are large normal mirrors that have a magnifying inset, and others to which a magnifying mirror is attached on an adjustable arm. Some mirrors double as doors to cabinets and many are framed by the outer rim of the bathroom door. A round or oval mirror makes an interesting alternative to the more traditional square or rectangular mirror. A round mirror can also be used to mimic a porthole in a bathroom with a nautical theme.

If you have plenty of wall space in the bathroom, try to put soap trays and shelves near where they are needed. For example, an open-mesh wire-

rimmed shelf is a practical accessory to have in a shower enclosure because the water can run through the open construction and the shelf will hold all the essentials in the appropriate place.

An old-fashioned accessory that survives because it does its job well is the classic bath rack. The open-mesh metal types allow water to drip off sponges, facecloths, and soaps and back into the bathtub.

A bathroom glass attached to the wall and a soap dish either resting on the basin or attached to the wall help to keep some of the clutter off the shelves. The "glass" may be a glass, plastic, or ceramic beaker held in a metal or plastic ring. The soap holder should be in a coordinated style.

Neatly stacked and folded, towels can bring color and texture to a bathroom. They come in all sorts of types and textures, ranging from coarser linen and natural cotton—which are invigorating after a morning shower and absorbent and light next to the skin—to velvet-pile towels that are thick and plush, and absorb water rather than stimulate the skin.

Toweling is often used for bathmats, which are generally chosen to coordinate with the color of the towels. Cork mats are also good, especially when you step out of the shower, since they feel soft and warm underfoot. Cork mats should be pretreated so they are water-resilient rather than absorbent. Another option is a duckboard, which is suitable only for a tiled or linoleum-covered floor because water will run straight through the open wooden framework onto the floor.

ABOVE **A curve of chrome attached to the wall by an invisible fixture makes an elegant roll holder.**

BELOW LEFT **A vertical bar with towel rods, a metal glass, and a shaving mirror is a neat storage idea for a small room.**

BELOW CENTER **The apparent fragility of this towel rod is deceptive, as a glass or acrylic rod of this thickness is remarkably strong. Fragile-looking items are pretty in a classic feminine bathroom.**

BELOW RIGHT **Even the most functional bathroom items can be stored attractively. This chrome toilet brush holder is neat and stylish.**

storage, furniture, and accessories notes

useful
addresses

The following pages contain extensive
lists of bathroom companies, suppliers,
and manufacturers of bathroom fixtures
and appliances, tiles and splashbacks,
flooring, and lighting. Pages 151 and 152
have been left blank for you to add contact
details of your own favorite sources.

bathroom fixtures and appliances

Alchemy Glass & Light
3143 South La Cienega
Los Angeles, CA 90016
t. 310 836 8631
f. 310 836 8631
Glass sinks.

**Alumax Bath
Enclosures**
1617 N. Washington
P.O. Box 40
Magnolia, AR 71753
t. 870 234 4260
f. 870 234 3181

American Standard
1 Centennial Ave
Piscataway, NJ 08855
t. 732 980 3000
f. 732 980 3335
www.americanstandard.
   com
*Tubs, whirlpools, sinks,
and toilets.*

**Aquarius by Praxis
Industries**
Rt. 1, Box 460, Industrial
Park
Savannah, TN 38372
t. 800 443 7269
f. 901 925 7656
*Acrylic/fiberglass bath
units.*

Baltic Leisure Co.
PO Box 530
601 Lincoln St
Oxford, PA 19363
t. 800 441 7147
f. 888 422 5842
www.balticleisure.com
*Sauna rooms, steam
baths, humidors.*

Basco Mfg Inc.
7201 Snider Road
Mason, OH 45040
t. 800 543 1938
f. 800 989 1919

**Burgess International
Bathroom Fixtures**
6810-B Metroplex
Romulus, MI 48174
t. 800 837 0092
f. 800 860 0093
www.burgess
   international.com
*Toilets, bidets, vanities,
traditional bathroom
furniture.*

Cameo Marble
540 Central Court
New Albany, IN 47150
t. 812 944 5055
f. 812 944 5236
*Cultured marble vanity
tops, tubs, showers.*

Capri Bath Products
131 Hudson Loop
El Dorado, AR 71730
t. 800 367 8035
f. 870 862 7312
*Shower pans, wall
surrounds.*

Diamond Spas Inc.
760 S. 104th St
Broomfield, CO 80020
t. 800 951 SPAS
f. 303 665 0173

Elkay Mfg Co.
2222 Camden Court
Oak Brook, IL 60523
t. 630 574 8484
www.elkay.com
Sinks, faucets.

**Gemini Bath &
Kitchen Products**
1501 E. Broadway
Tucson, AZ 85719
t. 520 770 0667
f. 520 770 9964
www.geminibkp.com
Showers, sinks.

**Gerber Plumbing
Fixtures Corp.**
4600 West Touhy Ave
Chicago, IL 60712
t. 847 675 6570
f. 847 675 5192
www.gerberonline.com
Toilets, bidets, faucets.

**Heritage Marble
of Ohio Inc.**
7086 Huntley Road
Columbus, OH 43229
t. 614 436 1464
f. 614 436 9874
*Custom-made marble,
onyx and granite
fixtures.*

HydraBaths
2100 South Fairview St
Santa Ana, CA 92704
t. 714 556 9133
f. 714 751 8652
www.hydrabaths.com
*Whirlpools, steam
cabinets.*

Hydro Systems
50 Moreland Road
Simi Valley, CA 93065
t. 805 584 9990
f. 805 584 8125
www.hydrosystem.com
*Whirlpools, bathtubs,
showers, shower pans.*

Interbath Inc.
665 N. Baldwin Park
Boulevard
City of Industry
CA 91746
t. 626 369 1841
f. 626 961 3534
www.interbath.com
Shower systems.

Jacuzzi Whirlpool Bath
2121 North California
Boulevard, Suite 475
Walnut Creek, CA 94596
t. 925 938 7070
f. 925 256 1749
www.jacuzzi.com
*Whirlpools, shower
systems.*

Kallista Inc.
2446 Verna Ct
San Leandro, CA 94577
t. 510 899 6680
www.kallistainc.com

Kohler Co.
444 Highland Drive
Kohler, WI 53044
t. 800 4 KOHLER
f. 920 459 1623
www.kohlerco.com
*Bathroom suites in a
wide range of styles.*

LASCO Bathware
3255 East Miraloma Ave
Anaheim, CA 92806
t. 800 877 2005
f. 714 528 1161
*Acrylic fixtures, shower
doors.*

Lubidet USA Inc.
1980 South Quebec St,
#104
Denver, CO 80231
t. 800 582 4338
f. 303 368 0810
Bidets.

Luxury Bath Systems
232 James St
Bensenville, IL 60106
t. 800 354 2284
f. 630 595 4483

MAAX Inc.
600 Rte Cameron
Ste-Marie-de-Bce
Que, CAN G6E 1B2
t. 418 387 4155
f. 418 387 3507
Showers, tubs,
whirlpools.

Marble Madness
1430 S. Mint St, Suite C
Charlotte, NC 28703
t. 704 343 2458
f. 704 331 8678
www.marblemadness.com
Mosaic sinks, stone
mirror frames.

Mirolin Industries Inc.
60 Shorncliffe Road
Toronto
Ontario, CAN M8Z 5K1
t. 416 231 9030
f. 416 231 0929
Showers, tubs,
enclosures.

Mister Miser Urinals
4901 North 12th St
Quincy, IL 62301
t. 888 228 6900
f. 217 228 6906
www.MisterMiser.com
Residential urinals.

MTI Whirlpools
670 N. Price Road
Sugar Hill, GA 30518
t. 800 783 TUBS
f. 800 GET TUBS
www.mtiwhirlpools.com

Pearl Baths
9224 73rd Ave N.
Minneapolis, MN 55428
t. 612 424 3335
f. 612 424 9808
www.pearlbaths.com
Whirlpools.

PDC Spas & Baths
P.O. Box 4007
Williamsport, PA 17701
t. 800 451 1420
f. 570 323 8485
Stainless-steel fixtures.

ProMark, L.L.C.
2070 Irwin Circle
Las Vegas, NV 89119
t. 702 696 9677
f. 702 696 0886
Toilets, bidets, tubs,
whirlpools.

PS Craftsmanship Corp.
10-40 Jackson Ave
Long Island City
NY 11101
t. 718 729 3686
f. 718 729 3781
Wooden lavs, vanities,
tubs.

Royal Baths Mfg Co.
14635 Chrisman Road
Houston, TX 77039
t. 281 442 3400
f. 281 442 1455
www.royalbaths.com
Whirlpools, shower
bases, shower seats,
toilets.

Sherle Wagner
60 East 57th St
New York, NY 10022
t. 212 758 3300
f. 212 207 8010
www.sherlewagner.com

Shower Shapes
51 Cass Pl.
Goleta, CA 93117
t. 800 316 4989
f. 805 639 4012

Sussman Lifestyle
Group
43—20 34th St
Long Island City
NY 11101
t. 800 76STEAM
f. 718 472 3256
www.mrsteam.com
Steam baths, saunas.

Swan Corp.
One City Center
23rd floor
St Louis, MO 63101
t. 314 231 8148
f. 314 231 8165
www.theswancorp.com
Shower systems, solid
surfaces.

SWC Industries Inc.
1505 Industrial Drive
Henderson, TX 75652
t. 800 999 1459
f. 903 657 8197
Acrylic whirlpools,
shower bases.

Thermasol
2255 Union Place
Simi Valley, CA 93065
t. 800 631 1601
f. 805 579 8765
www.thermasol.com
Steam baths, saunas,
heaters, fog-free
mirrors.

Thermo Spas Inc.
155 East St
Wallingford, CT 06492
t. 203 265 6133
f. 203 265 7133
Portable whirlpools, hot
tubs.

Toto USA
1155 Southern Road
Morrow, GA 30260
t. 770 282 8686
f. 770 968 8697
www.totousa.com

Tower Industries
655 Third St NW
Massillon, OH 44647
t. 330 837 2216
f. 330 837 2642

TubMaster Corp
413 Virginia Drive
Orlando, FL 32803
t. 407 898 2881
f. 407 898 3856

Waterworks
185 Steele St
Denver, CO 80206
t. 800 998 2284
www.waterworks.com
Fixtures, fittings, tiles.

Whitehaus Collection
589 Orange Ave
Westhaven, CT 06516
t. 800 527 6690
f. 800 694 4837
www.whitehaus
   collection.com
Specialty bathroom
products.

fittings and accessories

Allied Brass Mfg Co.
149 Wooster St
New York, NY 10012
t. 212 674 1597
f. 212 353 0837
Solid brass accessories.

Baldwin Hardware Corp
P.O. Box 15048
Reading, PA 19612
t. 610 777 7811
f. 610 775 5564
Solid brass accessories, decorative hardware.

Bed, Bath & Beyond
620 6th Avenue
New york, NY 10011
800 GO BEYOND
www.bedbathandbeyond.
   com
Modern bathroom accessories.

The Chicago Faucet Co.
2100 S. Clearwater Drive
Des Plaines, IL 60018
t. 847 803 5000
f. 847 803 4499
Faucets.

Colonial Bronze Co
511 Winstead Road
Torrington, CT 06790
t. 860 489 9233
f. 860 482 8760
Accessories, decorative hardware.

Crate & Barrel
646 N Michigan Avenue
Chicago, IL 60611
For a retailer near you:
t. 800 927 9202
www.crateandbarrel.com
Contemporary accessories.

Delta Faucet Co.
55 E. 111th St
Indianapolis, IN 46280
t. 317 848 1812
f. 317 573 3486
www.deltafaucet.com
Faucets.

DK Heating Systems Inc.
587 North Edgewood Ave
Wood Dale, IL 60191
t. 630 787 0887
f. 630 787 0572
Floor-warming systems, towel warmers, fog-free mirrors.

Epanel Inc.
P.O. Box 115
Pennington, NJ 08534
t. 800 537 2635
f. 609 466 0773
Electric towel warmers, towel bars, towel rings.

Foremost Industries
906 Murray Road
East Hanover, NJ 07936
t. 973 428 0400
f. 973 428 6166
Faucets, vanities, vitreous china.

The French Reflection Inc.
8901 Beverly Boulevard
Los Angeles, CA 90048
t. 310 659 3800
f. 310 652 8494
Task mirrors.

Hansa
1432 West 21st St
Chicago, IL 60608
t. 800 343 4431
Designer faucets.

Hansgrohe Inc.
1465 Ventura Drive
Cumming, GA 30040
t. 800 719 1000
www.hansgrohe.com
European-style faucets.

Ikea
U.S. Flagship location:
1800 East McConnor
Parkway
Schaumburg, IL 60173
Mail order and online
www.ikea.com
Home basics at great prices.

ITC Inc.
230 E. Lakewood
Boulevard, P.O. Box 8338
Holland, MI 49422
t. 616 396 1355
f. 616 396 1152
Faucets, accessories.

JADO Bathroom & Hardware Mfg Co.
7845 E. Paradise Ln.
Scottsdale, AZ 85260
t. 480 991 2675
f. 480 951 7165
Luxury faucets and accessories.

Kroin Inc.
180 Fawcett St
Cambridge, MA 02138
t. 617 492 4000
f. 617 492 4001
Towel bars and accessories.

KWC Faucets
1770 Corporate Drive
Suite 580
Norcross, GA 30093
t. 888 592 3287
Faucets.

Moen Inc.
25300 Al Moen Drive
North Olmstead
OH 44070
t. 440 962 2000
f. 440 962 2770
www.moen.com
Water-filtering faucet, shower controls.

Restoration Hardware
935 Broadway
New York, NY10011
t. 212 260 9479
www.restorationhardware.
   .com
Traditional accessories.

Robern
701 N. Wilson Ave
Bristol, PA 19007
t. 215 826 9800
f. 215 826 9633
www.robern.com
Mirrored cabinetry, lighting, mirrors.

Safetek International Inc.
4340 Fortune Pl., Unit A
West Melbourne
FL 32904
t. 407 952 1300
f. 800 967 2766
Safety bars, shower seats.

Shower Solutions Inc.
3139 W. Holcombe, #635
Houston, TX 77025
t. 713 661 9088
f. 713 669 8454
Shower curtain rods.

Siro Designs Inc.
10301 NW 50th St
Suite 111
Sunrise, FL 33351
t. 954 749 1155
f. 954 749 9745
www.sirodesigns.com
Decorative hardware.

TFI Corp
1065 Marauder Street
Chico, CA 95973
t. 530 891 6390
f. 530 893 1273
www.tficorp.com
Corian products.

lighting and miscellaneous

LIGHTING

Alkco Lighting
11500 Melrose Ave
Franklin Park, IL 60131
t. 847 451 0700
f. 847 451 7512
www.alkco-lighting.com
Undercabinet lighting.

American Lighting Inc.
7660 E. Jewell Ave, Unit C
Denver, CO 80231
t. 800 880 1180
r. 303 695 7633

The Basic Source
655 Carlson Court
Rohnert Park, CA 94928
t. 800 428 0044
Contract-quality lighting fixtures and wall sconces.

Con-Tech Lighting
3865 Commercial Ave
Northbrook, IL 60062
T. 847 559 5500
F. 847 559 5505
www.con-
    techlighting.com

DURO-LITE Lighting
4101 W. 123rd St
Alsip, IL 60803
t. 800 720 DURO
f. 708 371 0627
Halogen undercabinet lighting.

Electrics Lighting and Design
530 West San Francisco
Suite H
San Rafael, CA 94901
t. 415 258 9996
More than 100 lighting lines, most from Italy.

Hafele America Co.
3901 Cheyenne Drive
P.O. Box 4000
Archdale, NC 27263
t. 800 334 1873
www.hafeleonline.com
Specialty lighting.

Hunter Fan
2500 Frisco Avenue
Memphis, TN 38114
t. 800 448 6837
www.hunterfan.com
Silent ceiling fans, many of which incorporate built-in lighting.

Lumax Industries Inc.
Chestnut Ave & 4th St
Altona, PA 16603
t. 814 944 2537
f. 814 944 6413
Fluorescent lighting products.

MSK Illuminations
969 Third Avenue
New York, NY 10022
t. 212 888 6474
All types of lighting.

NuLite
7001 East 57th Place
Commerce City
CO 80022
t. 303 287 9646
www.nulite.net
A wide variety of lighting solutions includes popular fluorescent fixtures.

Period Lighting Fixtures
167 River Road
Clarksburg, MA 01247
t. 413 664 7141
f. 413 664 0312
Hand-crafted reproductions of period lighting designs.

Progress Lighting
P.O. Box 5704
Spartanburg, SC 29034
t. 864 599 6000
f. 864 599 6151
www.progresslighting.
    com
All types of lighting.

Task Lighting Corp.
P.O. Box 1090
Kearney, NE 68848
t. 800 445 6404
f. 308 234 9401
Low-voltage task and accent lighting.

Top Brass
3502 Parkdale Avenue
Baltimore, MD 21211
t. 800 359 4135
www.antiquelighting
    fixture.com
Unique lines ranging from antique reproductions to contemporary.

W.A.C. Lighting Co.
113—25 14th Avenue
College Point, NY 11356
t. 800 526 2588
f. 800 526 2585
www.wac.lighting.com
Recessed and undercabinet lighting.

MISCELLANEOUS

DreamMaker Bath and Kitchen by Worldwide
1020 North University
Parks Drive
Waco, TX 76707
t. 800 253 9153
f. 254 745 2588
Bathroom remodeling service.

Hydravac Corp.
P.O. Box 543042
Dallas, TX 75354
t. 972 745 2284
f. 972 745 2285
www.hydravac.com
Whirlpool bath cleaning equipment.

National Kitchen and Bath Association
687 Willow Grove St
Hackettstown, NJ 07840
t. 908 852 0033
f. 908 852 1695
www.nkba.org

Perma Ceram Enterprises Inc.
65 Smithtown Boulevard
Smithtown, NY 11787
t. 800 645 5039
f. 516 724 9626
Tub, toilet, tile, and sink resurfacing.

Slip Tech
1111 LaMesa Ave
Spring Valley, CA 91977
t. 800 867 5470
f. 619 698 8978
Anti-slip materials.

Stone Care International Inc.
P.O. Box 703
Owings Mills, MD 21117
t. 800 839 1654
f. 800 SCI 6646
www.stonecare.com
Sealing, cleaning, polishing products for stone surfaces.

TR Industries Inc.
11022 Vulcan St
South Gate, CA 90280
t. 562 923 0838
f. 562 861 3475
Bath care products.

surfaces

FLOORING

Alcalayres America
8530 NW 70th Street
Miami, FL 33166
t. 877 640 0555
f. 305 640 0266
Porcelain and wall tiles.

American Marazzi Tile
359 Clay Road
Sunnyvale, TX 75182
T. 972 226 0110
F. 972 226 2263
Glazed floor and wall tiles.

Ann Sacks Tile & Stone
8120 NE 33rd Drive
Portland, OR 97211
t. 800 278 TILE
www.annsackstile.com
Limestone, terra-cotta, marble, mosaics, handcrafted tile, stone antiquities.

Armstrong World Industries Inc.
2500 Columbia Ave
Lancaster, PA 17604
t. 717 569 2259
f. 717 396 6334
www.armstrongfloors.
    com
Vinyl and laminate flooring.

Batik Tile
69 Bralan Court
Gaithersburg, MD 20877
t. 888 MYBATIK
f. 301 990 0009
Hand-painted and decorative tiles.

Bisazza
8530 NW 30th Terrace
Miami, FL 33122
t. 305 597 4099
f. 305 597 9844
www.bisazzausa.com
Italian-made mosaic and terrazzo tiles.

Chemetal Corp
10 Research Drive
Stratford, CT 06497
t. 203 375 5300
f. 203 377 5298
Decorative metallic surfaces.

Country Floors Inc.
8735 Melrose Avenue
Los Angeles, CA 90069
t. 310 657 0510
www.countryfloors.com
Handcrafted, decorative art tiles; limestone and travertine; mosaics.

Dakota Granite
14964 484th Ave
P.O. Box 1351
Millbank, SD 57252
t. 800 843 3333
f. 800 338 5346
www.dakgran.com
Granite floors.

Florenata Solid Surfaces
2921 NW Commerce
Park Drive
Boynton Beach, FL 33426
t. 561 540 4411
f. 561 540 4466
Solid surface sheets.

Gerbert
715 Fountain Avenue
P.O. Box 4944
Lancaster, PA 17406
t. 717 299 5035
Unusual recycled rubber flooring.

Glaazart USA
5949 Butterfield Road
Hillside, IL 60162
t. 708 449 9990
f. 708 449-9993
Ceramic floor and wall tiles.

Granitewerks Inc.
2218 North Elston Ave
Chicago, IL 60614
t. 773 292 1202
f. 773 292 1202
Natural stone.

Interceramic USA
2333 S. Jupiter Road
Garland, TX 75041
t. 214 503 5500
f. 214 503 4930
Ceramic floor and wall tiles.

Kentile Floors Inc.
1 Kentile Road
South Plainfield
NJ 07080
t. 908 757 3000
f. 908 757 8953
Vinyl composition flooring.

LG Decorative Surfaces
9940 Currie Davis Drive
Tampa, FL 33619
t. 813 627 0505
f. 813 620 4979
www.lgsurfaces.com.

Linoleum City
5657 Santa Monica Blvd
Hollywood, CA 90038
t. 213 469 0063
Selection of linoleum.

Lonseal
928 East 238th Street
Bldg A
Carson, CA 90745
t. 800 832 7111
Sheet vinyl flooring.

Mannington Floors
P.O. Box 30
Salem, NJ 08079
t. 800 443 5667
Sheet-vinyl and laminate flooring.

Norwegian Wood Inc.
30 Pen Hazlow St
Portsmouth, NH 03801
t. 800 250 WOOD
f. 603 436 7083

Paris Ceramics
1373 Merchandise Mart
Chicago, IL 60654
t. 312 464 9830
f. 312 464 9835
Antique limestone and terracotta, ceramics, mosaics.

PermaGrain Products Inc.
4789 West Chester Pike
Newtown Square
PA 19073
t. 610 353 8801
Natural wood flooring.

Portobello
1205 N. Miller
Anaheim, CA 92803
t. 714 234 2344
g. 714 234 4344
www.portobelloamerica.
    com
Ceramic wall and floor tiles.

PS Craftsmanship Corp.
10—40 Jackson Ave
Long Island City
NY 11101
t. 718 729 3686
f. 718 729 3781
Antique limestone and terracotta, ceramics, mosaics.

favorite shops and suppliers

name _____

address _____

_____

_____

tel _____

fax _____

e-mail _____

www _____

name _____

address _____

_____

_____

tel _____

fax _____

e-mail _____

www _____

name _____

address _____

_____

_____

tel _____

fax _____

e-mail _____

www _____

name _____

address _____

_____

_____

tel _____

fax _____

e-mail _____

www _____

name _____

address _____

_____

_____

tel _____

fax _____

e-mail _____

www _____

name _____

address _____

_____

_____

tel _____

fax _____

e-mail _____

www _____

name _____

address _____

_____

_____

tel _____

fax _____

e-mail _____

www _____

name _____

address _____

_____

_____

tel _____

fax _____

e-mail _____

www _____

favorite shops and suppliers

name
address

tel
fax
e-mail
www

name
address

tel
fax
e-mail
www

name
address

tel
fax
e-mail
www

name
address

tel
fax
e-mail
www

name
address

tel
fax
e-mail
www

name
address

tel
fax
e-mail
www

name
address

tel
fax
e-mail
www

name
address

tel
fax
e-mail
www

architects and designers whose work is featured in this book

Key: **a**=above, **b**=below, **c**=center, **l**=left, **r**=right

Azman Owens Architects
8 St Albans Place
London N1 0NX
t. +44 20 7354 2955
f. +44 20 7354 2966
Page **44 b**

Bataille + ibens Design N.V.
Architects
Vekestraat 13 Bus 14
2000 Antwerpen
Belgium
t. +32 3 213 8620
f. +32 3 213 8639
bataille.ibens@
planetinternet.be
Page **16**

Bedmar & Shi Designers Pte Ltd
12A Keong Saik Road
Singapore 089119
t. +65 2277 117
f. +65 2277 695
bedmar.shi@pacific.net.sg
A Singapore-based firm
established in 1980
specializing in residential
projects and in interior
design mainly for
restaurants and offices.
Page **15 l**

behun / ziff design
153 E. 53rd Street, 43rd Floor
New York, NY 10022
USA
t. 212 292 6233
f. 212 292 6790
Pages **39 l, 52–55**

Belmont Freeman Architects
Project team: Belmont
Freeman (Principal
designer), Alane Truitt,
Sangho Park
110 West 40th Street
New York, NY 10018
USA
t. 212 382 3311
f. 212 730 1229
Page **6, 19 a**

Bilhuber Inc.
330 East 59th Street
6th Floor
New York, NY 10022
USA
t. 212 308 4888
Pages **93 r, 97 r**

Bowles & Linares
32 Hereford Road
London W2 5AJ
t. +44 20 7229 9886
Page **115 a**

Brookes Stacey Randall
16 Winchester Walk
London SE1 9AQ
t. +44 20 7403 0707
f. +44 20 7403 0880
info@bsr-architects.com
www.bsr-architects.com
Pages **7, 45 l, 95, 106 bl, 108a, 109a**

Bruce Bierman Design, Inc.
29 West 15 Street
New York, NY 10011
USA
t. 212 243 1935
f. 212 243 6615
www.biermandesign.com
Pages **48–51**

CR Studio Architects, PC
6 West 18th Street, 9th Floor
New York NY 10011
USA
t. 212 989 8187
f. 212 924 4282
victoria@crstudio.com
www.crstudio.com
Pages **73 r, 99 a, 127 r, 141 c & r**

Carden Cunietti
83 Westbourne Park Road,
London W2 5QH
t. +44 20 7229 8559
f. +44 20 7229 8799
www.carden-cunietti.com
Pages **68–71, 113 br, 119 ar, 121 b, 127 c, 137 ar**

Carpenter Oak Ltd.
The Framing Yard
East Cornworthy
Totnes, Devon TQ9 7HF
t. 01803 732 900
f. 01803 732 901
Page **80 b**

Garth Carter
Specialist interiors painter
t. 0958 412953
Pages **46 l, 105 al, 122 ar**

Charles Bateson Design Consultants
Interior Design
18 Kings Road
Twickenham TW1 2QS
t. +44 20 8892 3141
f. +44 20 8891 6483
Charles.bateson@btinternet.com
Pages **101 l, 106 ar & c**

Chester Jones Ltd
Interior Design
240 Battersea Park Road
London SW11 4NG
t. +44 20 7498 2717
f. +44 20 7498 7312
chester.jones@virgin.net
Pages **9c, 27 r, 137 ac**

Christopher Leach Design Ltd
Interior Design
The Studio
13 Crescent Place
London SW3
t. +44 20 7235 2648
f. +44 20 7235 2669
mail@christopherleach.com
Pages **96 l, 107 r, 140 al**

Circus Architects
Unit 1
Summer Street
London EC1R 5BD
t. +44 20 7833 1999
Page **94 r**

Clive Butcher Designs
The Granary
The Quay, Wivenhoe
Essex CO7 9BU
t./f. 01206 827708
Pages **23 r, 88 r, 104**

Coburn Architecture
70 Washington Street
Studio 1001
Brooklyn, NY 11201
USA
t. +1 718 875 5052
f. +1 718 488 8305
info@coburnarch.com
www.coburnarch.com
Page **112 ar**

Anthony Collett
Collett Zarzycki Ltd.
Fernhead Studios
2b Fernhead Road
London W9 3ET
t. +44 20 8969 6967
f. +44 20 8960 6480
mail@czltd.co.uk
Page **26b**

Coskun Fine Art London
93 Walton Street
London SW3 2HP
t. +44 20 7581 9056
f. +44 20 7581 9056
gulgallery@aol.com
www.coskunfineart.com
Page **20 a & c**

DAD Associates
112–6 Old Street
London EC1V 9BD
t. +44 20 7336 6488
Page **85 r**

David Mikhail Architects
Unit 29
1–13 Adler Street
London E1 1EE
t. +44 20 7377 8424
f. +44 20 7377 5791
www.davidmikhail.com
Pages **87 ar & b, 92, 118 b**

Barbara Davis
t. +1 607 264 3673
Interior design; antique
hand-dyed linen, wool, and
silk textiles by the yard; soft
furnishings and clothes to
order.
Page **34 br**

Eric De Queker
DQ – Design In Motion
Koninklijkelaan 44
2600 Bercham, Belgium
Page **116**

Han Feng
Fashion Designer
333 West 39th Street
12th Floor
New York, NY 10018
USA
t. 212 695 9509
Page **25**

Filer & Cox
Architectural Deviants
194 Bermondsey Street
London SE1 3TQ
t. +44 20 7357 7574
f. +44 20 7357 7573
iru@filerandcox.com
www.filerandcox.com
Pages **89 l, 90 b**

Andy Martin of
Fin Architects and Designers
73 Wells Street
London W1P 3RD
finbox@globalnet.co.uk
Page **45 r**

Ken Foreman
Architect
105 Duane Street
New York NY 10007
USA
t./f. 212 924 4503
Page **75**

Frances Robinson Detail
Jewellery designers and
consultants
t. 0207 582 9564
f. 0207 587 3783
Page **9r**

Ory Gomez
Didier Gomez
Interior Design
15 rue Henri Heine
75016 Paris, France
t. +33 01 44 30 8823
f. +33 01 45 25 1816
orygomez@free.fr
Pages **106 al, 140 bl**

HM2
Architects: Richard
Webb, Project Director;
Andrew Hanson, Director
33–37 Charterhouse Square
London EC1M 6EA
t. +44 20 7600 5151
f. +44 20 7600 1092
andrew.hanson@
harper-mackay.co.uk
Page **101 r, 107, 113 bc, 123
bl**

William R. Hefner AIA
William Hefner Architect
L.L.C.
5820 Wiltshire Boulevard
Suite 601
Los Angeles, CA 90036
USA
t. +1 323 931 1365
f. +1 323 931 1368
wh@williamhefner.com
www.williamhefner.com
Pages **18 al, 19b, 78, 111 br**

Sera Hersham-Loftus
'Rude' designer &
lampshade maker
t. +44 20 7286 5948
Pages **117 ar, 122 b**

Sarah Featherstone of
**Hudson Featherstone
Architects**
49–59 Old Street
London EC1V 9HX
t. +44 20 7490 5656
Pages **73 c, 91 a**

IPL Interiors
25 Bullen Street
London SW11 3ER
t. +44 20 7978 4224
f. +44 20 7978 4334
Page **143 c**

Gavin Jackson
Architect
m. 0705 0097561
Page **5**

John Barman Inc.
Interior Design &
Decoration
500 Park Avenue
New York, NY 10022
USA
t. 212 838 9443
john@barman.com
www.johnbarman.com
Page **123 a**

John Minshaw Designs Ltd
t. +44 20 7258.0627
f. +44 20 7258 0628
Pages **84, 103**

Eva Johnson
Interior Designer
t. 01638 731 362
f. 01638 731 855
Distributor of TRIP-TRAP
wood floor treatment
products.
Page **30**

Johnson Naylor
13 Britton Street
London EC1M 5SX
t. +44 20 7490 8885
f. +44 20 7490 0038
brian.johnson@
johnsonnaylor.co.uk
Page **14a**

**KRD–Kitchen Rogers
Design**
t. +44 20 8944 7088
ab@krd.demon.co.uk
Page **123 br**

**Laura Bohn Design
Associates, Inc.**
30 West 26th Street
New York, NY 10010
USA
t. 212 645 3636
f. 212 645 3639
Pages **92 l, 137 al & b**

Marino + Giolito
161 West 16th Street
New York NY 10011
USA
t./f. 212 675 5737
Pages **77, 105 br**

Paul Mathieu
Interior Design
France:
12 rue Matheron
13100 Aix-en-Provence
t. +33 4 42 23 97 77
f. +33 4 42 23 97 59
USA:
7 East 14th Street, # 805
New York, NY 10003
t. +1 646 638 4531
Pages **112 b, 130**

Frédéric Méchiche
4 rue de Thorigny
75003 Paris, France
Pages **24 l, 85 l**

Jean-Louis Ménard
Architect
t./f. +33 1 46 34 44 92
Pages **56–59, 105 bl, 122 al**

Moneo Brock Studio
Architecture & Interior
Design
371 Broadway, 2nd Floor
New York, NY 10013
USA
t. 212 625 0308
f. 212 625 0309
www.moneobrock.com
Pages **82, 114 a**

Clare Mosley
Gilding, églomisé panels,
lamps
t. +44 20 7708 3123
Pages **73 l, 80 a**

Elie Mouyal
Architect
Rue Saâd Bnou Oubada n°
336 ISSIL
Boîte Postale N° 3667
Amerchich
Marrakech
Morocco
t. +212 4 30 05 02
Page **23 l**

**Mullman Seidman
Architects**
Architecture & Interior
Design
443 Greenwich Street, # 2A
New York, NY 10013
USA
t. 212 431 0770
f. 212 431 8428
msa@mullmanseidman.com
www.mullmanseidman.com
Pages **1, 39 r, 64–67, 133 b**

François Muracciole
Architect
54 rue de Montreuil
75011 Paris, France
t. +33 1 43 71 33 03
francois.muracciole@
libertysurf.fr
Page **124 bl**

**Nancy Braithwaite
Interiors**
2300 Peachtree Road
Suite C101, Atlanta
Georgia 30309
USA
Page **34 bl**

**Nasser Nakib Architect &
Bunny Williams Inc.**
Decorator
306 East 61st Street
Fifth Floor
New York, NY 10021
USA
t. 212 759 1515
f. 212 759 1612
Page **22**

Mona Nerenberg
Bloom
43 Madison Street
Sag Harbor, NY 11963
USA
t. +1 631 725 4680
Home & garden products
and antiques
Page **80 c**

Orefelt Associates
Design team: Gunnar
Orefelt, John Massey,
Gianni Botsford, Jason
Griffiths
4 Portobello Studios
5 Haydens Place
London W11 1LY
t. +44 20 7243 3181
f. +44 20 7792 1126
orefelt@msn.com
Pages **12, 119 l, 125 b**

Caroline Paterson
Paterson Gornall Interiors
50 Lavender Gardens
London SW11 1DN
t. +44 20 7738 2530
f. +44 20 7652 0410
Pages **23 r, 88 r, 104**

Michèle Rédélé
Interior Designer
90 Boulevard Malegerbes
Paris 75008, France

Johanne Riss
Stylist, designer and
fashion designer
35 Place du Nouveau
Marché aux Graens
1000 Brussels, Belguim
t. +32 2 513 0900
f. +32 2 514 3284
Page **86 b**

Roderick James Architects
Seagull House
Dittisham Mill Creek
Dartmouth, Devon TQ6 0HZ
Page **80 b**

Roger Oates Design
Rugs and runners
Shop & Showroom:
1 Munro Terrace
off Cheyne Walk
London SW10 0DL
Studio Shop:
The Long Barn
Eastnor, Ledbury
Herefordshire HR8 1EL
Mail Order Catalogue:
t. 01531 631611
Page **89 r**

Charles Rutherfoord
51 The Chase
London SW4 0NP
Pages **11, 87 al**

SCDA Architects
10 Teck Lim Road
Singapore 088386
t. +65 324 5458
f. +65 324 5450
scda@cyberway.com.sg
Page **15r**

Sandy Davidson Design
Interior Design
1505 Viewsite Terrace
Los Angeles, CA 90069
USA
f. +1 320 659 2107
SandSandD@aol.com
Pages **18 al, 19b, 78, 111 br**

Sheppard Day Design
t. +44 20 7821 2002
Page **111 l**

**Sidnam Petrone Gartner
Architects**
Coty Sidnam, Bill Petrone
and Eric Gartner
136 West 21st Street
New York, NY 10011
USA
t. 212 366 5500
f. 212 366 6559
sidnampetr@aol.com
Page **110 l, 117 l**

Simon Conder Associates
Architects & Designers
Nile Street Studios
8 Nile Street,
London N1 7RF
t. +44 20 7251 2144
f. +44 20 7251 2145
simon@simonconder.co.uk
Pages **18 ar & b, 111 ar**

Nigel Smith
t. +44 20 7278 8802
n-smith@dircon.co.uk
Pages **113 a, 124 br**

Enrica Stabile
L'Utile E Il Dilettevole
via della Spiga, 46
Milan, Italy
t. +39 02 76 00 84 20
stabile@enricastabile.com
www.enricastabile.com
Pages **31 a & c, 37 a, 76 r,
105 ar**

Guy Stansfeld
Architect
t. +44 20 8962 8666
Page **131 b**

Seth Stein
Architect
15 Grand Union Centre
West Rowl
London W10 5AS
t. +44 20 8968 8581
f. +44 20 8968 8591
admin@sethstein.com
Pages **86 a, 113 bl, 145**

Stephen Turvil Architects
41 Avondale Rise
London SE15 4AJ
t. +44 20 7639 2212
Turv@space1.demon.co.uk
Pages **43 b, 141 bl**

**Stephen Varady
Architecture**
Studio 5, 102 Albion Street
Surry Hills
Sydney, NSW 2010
Australia
t. +61 2 9281 4825
Page **133 a**

Steven Learner Studio
307 Seventh Avenue
New York, NY 10001
USA
t. 212 741 8583
f. 212 741 2180
www.stevenlearnerstudio.com
Pages **44a, 136**

Studio Works
6775 Centinela Avenue
Building # 3
Culver City
California 90230
USA
t. +1 301 390 5051
f. +1 301 390 2763
Page **94 l**

**Stutchbury & Pape
Architecture + Landscape
Architecture**
4/364 Barrenjoey Road
Newport
NSW 2106
Australia
t. +61 2 9979 5030
f. +61 2 9979 5367
snpala@ozemail.com.au
Have a reputation for
innovative thinking and
environmental sensitivity.
The land, site and place are
seen as directives toward
the solution of formulating a
building.
Page **14**

Bruno Tanquerel
Artist
2 Passage St Sébastien
75011 Paris
France
t. +33 1 43 57 03 93
Pages **79 b, 105 bc**

**Tsao & McKown
Architects**
20 Vandam Street 10th floor
New York, NY 10013
USA
t. 212 337 3800
f. 212 337 0013
Pages **41, 119 br**

**Jeff Kirby / Urban Research
Lab.**
Ground Floor
Lime Wharf
Vyner Street
London E2 9DJ
t. +44 20 8709 9060
info@urbanresearchlab.com
www.urbanresearchlab.com
Pages **39 c, 60–63, 125 ar**

Urban Salon Ltd
Architects
Unit D, Flat Iron Yard
Ayres Street
London SE1 1ES
t. +44 20 7357 8800
Page **79 a & c**

VX design & architecture
www.vxdesign.com
vx@vxdesign.com
t./f. +44 20 7370 5496
Pages **9l, 13**

**Vicente Wolf Associates,
Inc.**
333 West 39th Street
New York, NY 10018
USA
Page **88 l**

Constanze von Unruh
Constanze Interior Projects
Interior Design
Richmond
Surrey
t. +44 20 8948 5533
constanze@constanze
interiorprojects.com
Pages **5 a, 21 b**

Heidi Wish and Philip Wish
Interior Design & Build
t./f. +44 20 7684 8789
m. 07710 283 611
Page **139 r**

Bonnie Young
Director of Global Sourcing
and Inspiration at Donna
Karan International
t. 212 228 0832
Page **24 r**

picture credits

All illustrations by Shonagh Rae

All photography by Chris Everard (unless stated otherwise)

Key: a=above, b=below, r=right, l=left, c=center, ph=photographer

Endpapers ph Chris Everard; 1 Suze Orman's apartment in New York designed by Patricia Seidman and Monika Brugger of Mullman Seidman Architects; 2 ph Polly Wreford/Ros Fairman's house in London; 3 a Gabriele Sanders' apartment in New York; 3 b ph Jan Baldwin; 4 ph Andrew Wood/Robert Kimsey's apartment in London designed by Gavin Jackson; 5 a ph Jan Baldwin/Constanze von Unruh's house in London; 5 b ph Andrew Wood; 6 ph Polly Wreford/an apartment in New York designed by Belmont Freeman Architects; 7 Freddie Daniells' apartment in London designed by Brookes Stacey Randall; 9 l Ian Chee of VX design & architecture; 9 c ph Jan Baldwin/Designer Chester Jones' house in London; 9 r ph Catherine Gratwicke/Frances Robinson & Eamonn McMahon's house in London; 11 ph Henry Bourne/a house in London designed by Charles Rutherfoord; 12 a house in Hampstead, London designed by Orefelt Associates; 13 Ian Chee of VX design & architecture; 14 a ph Andrew Wood /Roger and Suzy Black's apartment in London designed by Johnson Naylor; 14 b ph Jan Baldwin/Robert & Gabrielle Reeves' house in Clareville designed by Stutchbury & Pape Architecture + Landscape Architecture; 15 l ph Andrew Wood/'Melwani House' designed by Bedmar & Shi Designers in Singapore; 15 r ph Andrew Wood/a house at Jalan Berjaya, Singapore designed by Chan Soo Khian of SCDA Architects; 16 ph Andrew Wood/a house near Antwerp designed by Claire Bataille and Paul ibens; 17 ph Andrew Wood/Isosceles Land Pte Ltd's house in Singapore designed by Chan Soo Khian of SCDA Architects; 18 al & 19 b ph James Morris/'The Jackee' and Elgin Charles House in California's Hollywood Hills, designed by William R. Hefner AIA, interior design by Sandy Davidson Design; 18 ar & b ph James Morris/a loft apartment in London designed by Simon Conder Associates; 19 a ph Polly Wreford/an apartment in New York designed by Belmont Freeman Architects; 20 a & c ph Jan Baldwin/Art Dealer Gül Coskun's apartment in London; 21 a Sig.ra Venturini's apartment in Milan; 21 b ph Jan Baldwin /Constanze von Unruh's house in London; 22 an apartment in New York designed by Nasser Nakib Architect & Bunny Williams Inc. Decorator; 23 l ph Simon Upton; 23 r Philippa Rose's house in London designed by Caroline Paterson/Victoria Fairfax of Paterson Gornall Interiors, together with Clive Butcher Designs; 24 l ph Fritz von der Schulenburg/Frédéric Méchiche's apartment in Paris; 24 r ph Catherine Gratwicke/the brownstone in New York of Bonnie Young, director of global sourcing and inspiration at Donna Karan International; 25 ph Andrew Wood/Han Feng's apartment in New York designed by Han Feng; 26 a ph Andrew Wood/The Shell House, California, home of Chuck and Evelyn Plemons; 26 b ph Andrew Wood/Anthony & Julia Collett's house in London designed by Anthony Collett of Collett Zarzycki Ltd; 27 l ph Andrew Wood/the Caroline Deforest House in Pasadena, California, home of Michael Murray and Kelly Jones; 27 r ph Jan Baldwin/Designer Chester Jones' house in London; 28 a & 29 a Nadav Kander & Nicole Verity's house; 29 b ph Jan Baldwin; 30 ph Christopher Drake/Eva Johnson's house in Suffolk, interiors designed by Eva Johnson; 31 a & c ph Christopher Drake/Enrica Stabile's house in Le Thor, Provence; 31 b ph Henry Bourne; 32–33 ph Tom Leighton; 34 a ph Chris Tubbs/Vadim Jean's Thames sailing barge in London; 34 bl ph Simon Upton; 34 br ph

Christopher Drake/Designer Barbara Davis' own house in upstate New York; 35 ph Polly Wreford/Carol Reid's apartment in Paris; 36 a Catherine Gratwicke; 36 b ph Christopher Drake; 37 a ph Christopher Drake/Enrica Stabile's house in Le Thor, Provence; 37 b ph Henry Bourne; 39 l the Sugarman-Behun house on Long Island; 39 c Richard Oyarzarbal's apartment in London designed by Jeff Kirby of Urban Research Laboratory; 39 r ph Suze Orman's apartment in New York designed by Patricia Seidman and Monika Brugger of Mullman Seidman Architects; 41 Calvin Tsao & Zack McKown's apartment in New York designed by Tsao & McKown; 42 l ph Debi Treloar/Ben Johns & Deb Waterman Johns' house in Georgetown; 42 r ph Debi Treloar; 43 Alison Thompson & Billy Paulett's house in London designed by Stephen Turvil Architects; 44 a ph Debi Treloar/an apartment in New York designed by Steven Learner Studio; 44 b Andrew Wilson's house in London designed by Azman Owens; 45 l ph Ray Main/an apartment in London designed by Brookes Stacey Randall; 45 r Tiffany Ogden's house in London designed by Andy Martin of Fin Architects & Designers; 46 l Emma & Neil's house in London, walls painted by Garth Carter; 46 r an apartment in Milan designed by Daniela Micol Wajskol, Interior Designer. Wall sconces from Carati, Milan. Wooden towel rail from L'Utile e il Dilettevole, Milan; 48–51 "Manhattan Loft" designed by Bruce Bierman Design, Inc.; 52–55 the Sugarman-Behun house on Long Island; 56–59 Suzanne Slesin & Michael Steinberg's apartment in New York, design by Jean-Louis Ménard; 60 ph Alan Williams/Richard Oyarzarbal's apartment in London designed by Urban Research Laboratory; 61–63 bl Richard Oyarzarbal's apartment in London designed by Urban Research Laboratory; 63 br ph Alan Williams/Richard Oyarzarbal's apartment in London designed by Urban Research Laboratory; 64 l & 65 b ph Christopher Drake/Suze Orman's apartment in New York designed by Patricia Seidman and Monika Brugger of Mullman Seidman Architects; 64 r & 66–67 Suze Orman's apartment in New York designed by Patricia Seidman and Monika Brugger of Mullman Seidman Architects; 68–71 Mr & Mrs Jeremy Lascelles' house in London designed by Carden & Cunietti; 73 l ph Jan Baldwin/Clare Mosley's house in London; 73 c ph Henry Bourne/Dan & Claire Thorne's town house in Dorset designed by Sarah Featherstone; 73 r ph Jan Baldwin /Olivia Douglas & David DiDomenico's apartment in New York, designed by CR Studio Architects, PC; 75 ph Polly Wreford/Kathy Moskal's apartment in New York designed by Ken Foreman; 76 l ph Andrew Wood/Pete & Connie di Girolamo house in San Diego, California; 76 r ph Christopher Drake/Enrica Stabile's house in Le Thor, Provence; 77 New York City apartment designed by Marino + Giolito; 78 ph James Morris/'The Jackee' and Elgin Charles House in California's Hollywood Hills, designed by William R. Hefner AIA, interior design by Sandy Davidson Design; 79 a & c Gomez/Murphy Loft, Hoxton, London designed by Urban Salon Ltd; 79 b a house in Paris designed by Bruno Tanquerel; 80 a ph Jan Baldwin/Clare Mosley's house in London; 80 c ph Jan Baldwin/Mona Nerenberg and Lisa Bynon's house in Sag Harbor; 80 b ph Jan Baldwin/Roderick & Gillie James' house in Devon designed by Roderick James Architects and built by Carpenter Oak & Woodland Co. Ltd; 81 ph James Merrell; 82 ph Alan Williams/Hudson Street Loft in New York designed by Moneo Brock Studio; 84 a house in London designed by John Minshaw; 85 l ph Henry Bourne/Frédéric Méchiche's apartment in Paris; 85 r ph Henry Bourne/a loft in London designed by DAD Associates; 86 a a house in London by Seth Stein; 86 b ph Andrew Wood /Johanne Riss' house in Brussels; 87 al ph James Merrell/an apartment in London designed by Charles Rutherfoord; 87 ar & b Simon Brignall & Christina Rosetti's loft apartment in London designed by David Mikhail Architects; 88 l ph Fritz von der Schulenburg/Michael & Ruth Burke's plantation in Mississippi designed by Vicente Wolf of Vicente Wolf Associates Inc.; 88 r

Philippa Rose's house in London designed by Caroline Paterson /Victoria Fairfax of Paterson Gornall Interiors, together with Clive Butcher Designs; 89 l designed by Filer & Cox, London; 89 r ph Andrew Wood/Roger Oates and Fay Morgan's house in Eastnor; 90 a ph Henry Bourne/floor by Dalsouple, First Floor; 90 b designed by Filer & Cox, London; 91 a ph Henry Bourne/Dan and Claire Thorne's town house in Dorset designed by Sarah Featherstone; 92 Simon Brignall & Christina Rosetti's loft apartment in London designed by David Mikhail Architects; 93 l ph Ray Main/an apartment in New York designed by Laura Bohn Design Associates Inc., light from Lightforms; 93 r ph Ray Main/a house in Pennsylvania designed by Jeffrey Bilhuber; 94 l ph Ray Main/Andrea Luria and Zachary Feuer's house in Los Angeles designed by Studio Works, Robert Mangurian and Mary-Ann Ray; 94 r ph Ray Main/a loft in London designed by Circus Architects; 95 ph Ray Main/an apartment in London designed by Brookes Stacey Randall; 96 l ph Jan Baldwin/Christopher Leach's apartment in London; 96 r ph Tom Leighton; 97 l ph Ray Main; 97 r ph Ray Main/a house in Pennsylvania designed by Jeffrey Bilhuber, light by Hansen Lighting from Hinson & Co; 98 a ph Tom Leighton; 98 b ph Henry Bourne; 99 a ph Jan Baldwin/Olivia Douglas & David DiDomenico's apartment in New York, designed by CR Studio Architects, PC; 101 l Charles Bateson's house in London; 101 c One New Inn Square, a private dining room and home of chef David Vanderhook, all enquiries +44 20 7729 3645; 101 r Richard Hopkin's apartment in London designed by HM2; 103 John Minshaw's house in London designed by John Minshaw; 104 Philippa Rose's house in London designed by Caroline Paterson/Victoria Fairfax of Paterson Gornall Interiors, together with Clive Butcher Designs; 105 al Emma & Neil's house in London, walls painted by Garth Carter; 105 ar ph Christopher Drake/Enrica Stabile's house in Le Thor, Provence; 105 bl Suzanne Slesin & Michael Steinberg's apartment in New York designed by Jean-Louis Ménard; 105 bc an apartment in Paris designed by Bruno Tanquerel; 105 br New York City apartment designed by Marino + Giolito; 106 al ph Jan Baldwin/Interior Designer Didier Gomez's apartment in Paris; 106 ar & c Charles Bateson's house in London; 106 bl Freddie Daniells' apartment in London designed by Brookes Stacey Randall; 106 br Frazer Cunningham's house in London; 107 l Richard Hopkin's apartment in London designed by HM2; 107 r ph Jan Baldwin/Christopher Leach's apartment in London; 108 a & 109 a Freddie Daniells' apartment in London designed by Brookes Stacey Randall; 108 b ph Chris Tubbs; 109 b ph Henry Bourne; 110 l an apartment in New York designed by David Deutsch & Sidnam Petrone Gartner Architects; 110 r One New Inn Square, a private dining room and home of chef David Vanderhook, all enquiries +44 20 7729 3645; 111 l the London apartment of the Sheppard Day Design Partnership; 111 ar ph James Morris/a loft apartment in London designed by Simon Conder Associates; 111 br ph James Morris/'The Jackee' and Elgin Charles House in California's Hollywood Hills, designed by William R. Hefner AIA, interior design by Sandy Davidson Design; 112 al ph Jan Baldwin/David Gill's house in London; 112 ar ph Jan Baldwin/a house in New York designed by Brendan Coburn and Joseph Smith from Coburn Architecture; 112 b Jacques & Laurence Hintzy's apartment near Paris designed by Paul Mathieu; 113 ar architect Nigel Smith's apartment in London; 113 bl John Eldridge's loft apartment in London designed by Seth Stein; 113 bc Richard Hopkin's apartment in London designed by HM2; 113 br Paul Brazier & Diane Lever's house in London designed by Carden & Cunietti; 114 a Hudson Street Loft in New York designed by Moneo Brock Studio; 115 a ph Andrew Wood/a house in London designed by Bowles and Linares; 116 Eric De Queker's apartment in Antwerp; 117 l an apartment in New York designed by David Deutsch & Sidnam Petrone Gartner Architects; 117 ar Sera Hersham-Loftus' house in London; 117 br ph Polly Wreford/Carol Reid's apartment in Paris; 118 a One New Inn Square, a private dining room and home of chef David Vanderhook, all enquiries +44 20 7729 3645; 118 b Simon Brignall & Christina Rosetti's loft apartment in London designed by David Mikhail Architects; 119 l a house in Hampstead, London designed by Orefelt Associates; 119 ar Paul Brazier & Diane Lever's house in London designed by Carden & Cunietti; 119 br Calvin Tsao & Zack McKown's apartment in New York designed by Tsao & McKown; 120 al ph Polly Wreford; 121 a ph Jan Baldwin/Emma Wilson's house in London; 121 b a house in London designed by Carden & Cunietti; 122 al Suzanne Slesin & Michael Steinberg's apartment in New York, designed by Jean-Louis Ménard; 122 ar Emma & Neil's house in London, walls painted by Garth Carter; 122 b Sera Hersham-Loftus' house in London; 123 a John Barman's Park Avenue Apartment; 123 bl Richard Hopkin's apartment in London designed by HM2; 123 br ph Debi Treloar/Ab Rogers & Sophie Braimbridge's House, London, designed by Richard Rogers for his mother. Furniture design by KRD–Kitchen Rogers Design; 124 bl François Muracciole's apartment in Paris; 124 br architect Nigel Smith's apartment in London; 125 al Stephan Schulte's loft apartment in London; 125 ar Richard Oyarzarbal's apartment in London designed by Jeff Kirby of Urban Research Laboratory; 125 b a house in Hampstead, London designed by Orefelt Associates; 127 l ph Andrew Wood; 127 c Paul Brazier & Diane Lever's house in London designed by Carden & Cunietti; 127 r ph Jan Baldwin/Olivia Douglas & David DiDomenico's apartment in New York, designed by CR Studio Architects, PC; 129 ph Debi Treloar/Vincent & Frieda Plasschaert's house in Brugge, Belgium; 130 Jacques & Laurence Hintzy's apartment near Paris designed by Paul Mathieu; 131 a ph Andrew Wood /Paula Pryke's house in London; 131 b a house in London designed by Guy Stansfeld; 132 l ph Polly Wreford/Mary Foley's house in Connecticut; 132 r ph Andrew Wood/Dawna & Jerry Walter's house in London; 133 a ph James Merrell/Linda Parham and David Slobam's apartment designed by Stephen Varady Architecture; 133 b designed by Mullman Seidman Architects; 134 ph Henry Bourne; 134 b & 135 a ph Andrew Wood/Dawna & Jerry Walter's house in London; 135 b ph Andrew Wood; 136 ph Andrew Wood/the loft of Peggy and Steven Learner designed by Steven Learner Studio; 137 al & b ph David Montgomery/Laura Bohn's apartment in New York designed by Laura Bohn Design Associates; 137 ac ph Jan Baldwin/Designer Chester Jones' house in London; 137 ar Paul Brazier & Diane Lever's house in London designed by Carden & Cunietti; 138 a & cl ph Catherine Gratwicke/Jeff McKay's apartment in New York; 138 cr ph Tom Leighton; 138 b ph Chris Tubbs/Daniel Jasiak's home near Biarritz; 139 l ph Andrew Wood; 139 r Heidi Wish & Philip Wish's apartment in London designed by Moutarde & Heidi Wish; 140 al ph Jan Baldwin/Christopher Leach's apartment in London; 140 bl ph Jan Baldwin/Interior Designer Didier Gomez's apartment in Paris; 141 bl Alison Thompson & Billy Paulett's house in London designed by Stephen Turvil Architects; 141 c & r ph Jan Baldwin/Olivia Douglas & David DiDomenico's apartment in New York, designed by CR Studio Architects, PC; 143 l a house in Holland Park, London; 143 c James Merrell/François Gilles & Dominique Lubar, IPL Interiors; 143 r ph Jan Baldwin; 145 a house in London by Seth Stein; 160 ph Andrew Wood

In addition to the designers and owners mentioned above, we would also like to thank Elie Mouyal, artist Yuri Kuper, Marilyn Phipps, Peter Beale, Nancy Braithwaite, Aleid Rontgen and Annette Brederode, Caroline & Michael Breet, Roxanne Beis, Mary Emmerling, Shiraz Maneksha, and Michèle Rédélé.

index

Numbers in **bold** refer to main entries; those in *italics* refer to captions.

A
accessories **138–41**, *138–41*
  contemporary style 21
addresses 146–50
alcoves 25, *28*
arches *23*
ash 87

B
basins **116–21**, *116–21*
  Belfast sinks *121*
  console *57*
  contemporary style 18
  corner 117
  dimensions 45
  pedestal 117
  shelf-mounted bowls 18, *18, 21, 52, 54*, 117–18, *118*
  stands 32
  surrounds *17*, 18, 27
  twin 32, 43, *46, 116, 136*
  vintage 31
  wall-mounted 117
  wide *44*
baskets, storage *139*
bateau bathtub 19, 24, *24*
bath preparations 139
bathtub racks 134, *139*
bathmats 141
bathtubs **104–9**, *104–9*
  bedrooms *26, 43*
  cast-iron 104, 105
  country style 31, 33
  dimensions 45
  freestanding 18–19, 25, *104*
  planning 43
  rolltop 18, *20*, 23, *25*, 31, *34, 105*, 107
  site-built 54
  traditional style 23–5
bedrooms, baths *26, 43*
Belfast basins *121*
bidets 44, *122–3*, **123**
  dimensions 45
blinds 27
bowl basins 18, *18, 21, 52, 54*, 117–18, *118*
budgeting **46–7**

C
cabinets
  custom-built *51*
  glass *58*
  mobile *130*, 131
  see also cupboards; storage
carpets 26, 85, *88*
cast-iron baths 104, 105
cedar 14
ceilings, high *58*
ceramic tiles 14, 76, *76*, 77
  basin surrounds 27
  country style *32*, 34–5, *35*
  floors 90
  suppliers 147–8
chairs 28, *136–7*, 137
chrome fittings 20
color schemes *56*, 58
  contemporary streamlined style 15, 21
  country style *31, 33*, 35–6
composite board surfaces 79
concrete
  basin surrounds *17*
  surfaces 14, *82*
  floors **88–9**
containers 139, *140*
contemporary streamlined style **12–21**
copper tubs *24*
Corian 104
cork
  bathmats 141
  flooring **85–6**
corner basins 117
costing **46–7**
country style **30–7**
cupboards *130–3*, 131, 136
  traditional style *26*
  see also cabinets; storage
curtains 27, *137*
showers 28

D
dados 35, 79, *80*
decking *87*
dimensions, fittings 45
doors, pocket 65, *65*
downlighters 16, *49*, 94, *94*
dressing rooms **48–51**
dual-purpose bathrooms **48–51**

E
electric showers 110
electrical work 93
elm 87
elongated elegance 56–9
Empire (bateau) baths 19, 24, *24*
enamelling, reconditioning 105
encaustic tiles 82

F
fabrics 27–8
family bathrooms 42, *42*
faucets
  basins *116–21*, **119–20**
  bathtubs *104–9*, **108**
  contemporary style 20
  designer *20*
  quality *62*
  spouts *106*, 108, 120
fixtures **101–25**
  contemporary style **17–20**, 21
  country style *32*, 36
  dimensions 45
  planning **43–5**
  quality *62*
  reclaimed *27*, 29, *32, 33*
  suppliers 147
  traditional style 25, *27*, 29
flooring **84–91**
  contemporary streamlined style 14
  country style 36
  suppliers 147–8
  traditional style 26, 29
  see also individual materials e.g. carpets; cork
fluorescent lamps *93*, 96
found materials *34*
furniture **136–7**, *136–7*
  country style 37
  suppliers 150

G
glass
  basin surrounds 27
  baths 107
  bricks *12*, 69, *69, 94*
  cabinets *58*
  countertops 48
  fittings *12*
  obscured *19*
  panels *14*

safety 76
screens *19*, 113
shelves 131–3
showers *18*, 20
sliding panels *49*
surfaces 14, *18*, **76–7**, *78*
tiles 82
walls *6*
granite surfaces 78

H
hardwoods 78
  flooring 87
  panelling 27
  surfaces 14, *14*
heated towel rods **124–5**, *124–5*
heating 23, 28

I
inset basins 117
iroko 78

L
laminated glass 76
large bathrooms, planning **48–51**
laundry hampers 134, *135*
layout
  contemporary streamlined 13–14, 20
light/heaters 96
lighting *45*, 67, **92–9**
  contemporary style 16–17
  natural *45, 52*, 93, *98*, 99
  suppliers 150
limestone *15, 16, 49, 52*, 53
  surfaces 78
  tiles *12*
linoleum 36, 87, *91*
loofahs 139
low-voltage lighting 94, *94*

M
maple *71*, 87
marble surfaces 77
  basin surrounds 27
medium-sized bathrooms **60–3**
merbau 78
minimalist style *12*, **52–3**
mirrors *57, 78, 80, 138*, 139–40
  lights *93*, 94–6, *94–8*
  surfaces *18*

acknowledgments

Vinny Lee would like to thank David Jones of Colourwash, Jenny Hildreth, and the Building Design Centre.

Maggie Stevenson would like to thank everyone involved in the location research and photography for finding such inspirational bathrooms and capturing them on film.